Your God Is Alive and Well and Appearing in Popular Culture

Your God
Is Alive and Well
and Appearing
in Popular Culture

by
JOHN WILEY NELSON

THE WESTMINSTER PRESS
Philadelphia

Book Design by Dorothy Alden Smith

Published by The Westminster Press®
Philadelphia, Pennsylvania

PRINTED IN THE UNITED STATES OF AMERICA

Library of Congress Cataloging in Publication Data

Nelson, John Wiley, 1939–
    Your God is alive and well and appearing in popular culture.

    Bibliography: p.
    1. United States—Popular culture. 2. United States
—Religion. I. Title.
E169.12.N39   301.2 973   76–26092
ISBN 0–664–24866–7

To Robert Ezzell

CONTENTS

Continued

Acknowledgments

The thesis I present is an original one, as far as I know. However, my view of popular culture as the ritual of American cultural religion and such diverse applications as I attempt are heavy with obligations. People often ask me, "When do you find time to watch all that television, go to all those movies, read all those magazines?" The truth is, I have help. The reference notes and bibliography will identify my specific sources. But such textbook techniques, though necessary, can never sufficiently acknowledge the more general debts, for insights and ideas, for suggestions motivating the direction of research, and for the categories that drew together whole areas of collected facts and figures. It is to these sources that I want now to draw attention.

First, I owe a massive debt to the Popular Culture Association. When I stumbled across their second annual meeting in Toledo in 1972, it was like putting on glasses for the first time. The world of popular culture came into a clear, sharp focus for me—and has been accumulating depth and texture ever since. The Association introduced me to two outstanding journals published by Bowling Green University's Popular Press: *The Journal of Popular Culture* and *The Journal of Pop-*

ular Film. The consistently high quality of these journals, and the stimulation of the annual meetings of the PCA, have, to a large extent, been adrenalin to the body of my study of American cultural religion. Also, through the Association I came to read John Cawelti's *The Six-Gun Mystique,* undoubtedly the best book ever written on popular culture in America, and to meet Jack Nachbar, a professor at Bowling Green University. Nachbar knows more about the Western than anybody has any right to know. His anthology, *Focus on the Western,* brings together some of the best material written on the Western form.

I wish to thank all those friends and relatives who read and criticized the manuscript at its various levels. My longtime buddy Bill Sharp took time out from his own writing career to help me with mine, and introduced me to the Travis McGee Series. Gratitude is owed as well to those students whose research papers and penetrating questioning of my thesis provided stimulation and feedback for my ideas. I should also say a word of appreciation to my wife, Anne, who though studying for a law career and raising three children during the whole time I was preparing the manuscript, never failed to lend the project support and encouragement.

Most of all, however, I owe acknowledgment and thanks to my personal friend and colleague Professor Robert Ezzell, of Pittsburgh Theological Seminary. We had talked about writing this book together. Much of its substance emerged in conversation with him and is a direct result of his incredible and often uncanny sensitivity to the cultural milieu. Besides Catholic layman William Kuhns, whose challenging book *Environmen-*

tal Man is now out of print, as far as I know Bob Ezzell is the only other professional Christian educator in higher education who "sees" the seriousness of what this book is describing. Without his continued confidence and support, I never could have brought this project to print. That ought to explain the dedication.

J.W.N.

Introduction

My wife considers television the scourge of Western civilization. That Sunday evenings have to be scheduled around *Columbo* and *Kojak* is evidence enough of a degeneration into mindlessness. The argument that such "waste of time" trivia is an appropriate subject for scholarly research she views as a conspiracy against all that is noble and uplifting in the human spirit. To convince her that copies of *Playboy* and *Viva* on the nightstand are there in the interest of more effective communication may be *the* epitome of lost causes. And how can I peddle the social significance of a John Wayne Western to a Bergman film buff like her without being patronizingly indulged, if not disdainfully dismissed?

Yet, brashly and without remorse, I ask you for the present to ignore great literature, fine art, and the classics in music and dance. You are invited instead to scrutinize affairs much closer to home: the television of the Nielsen ratings, the blockbuster popular films, the gritty twang of country music, the images of being male and female in America in *Ladies' Home Journal, Playboy, Cosmopolitan, Field & Stream,* and other popular magazines, and the hard-boiled romanticism of detective hero Travis McGee.

Why? For fun? Partly—why deny it? But also for a far more significant reason. Popular culture entertains, to be sure; it provides laughter, tears, thrills and excitement, and occasionally sexual stimulation. However, while we watch or read or listen we are not merely being entertained. Simultaneously the shared values we hold as Americans are being reaffirmed, dramatically— in the same way that the rituals of worship services undergird and reaffirm religious beliefs.

Institutional religions (Christianity, Judaism, Islam, etc.) do not hold worship services to give the believer a chance to challenge the beliefs and values of the religion. On the contrary, such services are mortar to the bricks of the faith. In the worship ritual all that is affirmed in the religion is integrated in a dramatic style, explicitly designed to more firmly establish the foundation of life-meaning advocated by the religion. The same case can be made for popular culture in America. The success of any unit of popular culture is directly proportionate to its ability to perform satisfactorily the religious function of affirming and supporting beliefs already held in the dominant American cultural belief system.

Popular culture is to what most Americans believe as worship services are to what the members of institutional religions believe. That, in a nutshell, is our thesis.

All religions offer a system of beliefs and values, but so does American society. And the set of beliefs and values offered by American culture are not beliefs and values to which we are converted. We grow up believing that they are true. That's part of what it means to be an American. In fact, we learn them so well that most of the time we are not even fully conscious that we believe them. Every time we watch TV, read popular magazines or detective fiction, listen to country music, go to the movies or professional sports events, we are having these American cultural beliefs and values reaffirmed. We are in fact attending worship services of the American cultural religion fifteen to twenty hours a week. In the following pages we will present a "belief-systems analysis" of American popular culture. That is a shorthand way of saying we will try to uncover the values Americans hold as part of their self-understanding as members of this society. We will look at these values in their interrelationships—hence the word "systems" in combination with the word "belief." Admittedly we use the words "belief" and "value" rather loosely and always, for this study, interchangeably.

We will proceed as follows. First, we will briefly spell out the general meanings attached to what we will call the dominant and subdominant American belief systems. This, in a sense, will give the conclusions in advance, so we will have some idea where we are going.

Fortunately, the dominant belief system in American life has found a normative ritual form of expression in "the Western." In no other type of mythological drama is this dominant American salvation myth more comprehensively fixed. So classic is the Western form that one of the paradigm ritual dramas is not set in the American West at all, but rather in North Africa. It is Michael Curtiz' *Casablanca* (1943). So, in Chapter 2, we will break open the Western form and attempt a tentative grasp of its working parts. Since the mid-1950's the American cultural belief system has been undergoing a change. This is evident in the emergence of the "anti-

Western." *High Noon, Bad Day at Black Rock, Hombre, Lonely Are the Brave, The Wild Bunch,* and *High Plains Drifter* are examples. An "anti-Western" is a film (or popular-culture unit) that modifies the ritual drama by criticizing the classic form, or that tells the story so as to alter the way we respond. Therefore, Chapter 3 will document the rise and fall of the "anti-Western," and will do so in terms of the categories we talk about in Chapter 2. While we investigate these major categories for our analysis, we will be doing a belief analysis of American popular films. Chapters 4 through 7 introduce us to other mediums of popular culture, and employ the categories of Chapters 2 and 3 to analyze their belief systems. Chapter 8 will attempt to summarize this material and draw conclusions. It will add, as well, some specific suggestions for future study and implementation of this material, particularly as it affects the life of the church.

1

American Cultural Religion:
THE CREED
OF POPULAR CULTURE

What does it mean to be an "American"? It means to share values and beliefs about life and its meaning. These beliefs concern evil and its source, deliverance, and visions of the fulfilled and happy human life. In fact, "culture" is the manifestation of a system of shared beliefs about life's predicaments and solutions. There are potentially as many sets of beliefs as there are people, for no two people think exactly alike. But functioning societies in their most stable periods of self-understanding and expression produce a single dominant set of values which unifies all the shared individual or small-group beliefs into one characteristic belief system. At that point, to be an American means to affirm that dominant set of values.

This dominant, distinctly "American" system of beliefs is the basis of the American cultural "religion." Those institutions normally called "religions" are explicit in announcing precisely what they believe and in scheduling the ritual dramas of reaffirmation, that is, the worship services. American cultural religion is much less recognizably explicit, but no less powerfully pervasive in our lives. It applies the same care and concern to provide time and place for its "worship" ceremonies of value reaffirmation. In this chapter, we attempt to describe the American "belief system" and mention some distinctive features of its various possible "worship ceremonies."

THE AMERICAN CULTURAL BELIEF SYSTEM

It will be helpful to make a couple of introductory remarks concerning "belief systems" in general. First, a belief system is a systematically arranged set of answers to basic life-problem questions. All such answers are directed toward the resolving of unsatisfactory present experience in the direction of optimum fulfillment. This resolution occurs by means of an attack by some special, quasi-divine source of goodness and grace upon the source of dissatisfaction with the present. This attack is definitive, at least in ritual drama, and therefore eschatological—that is, it ushers in a final state of perfected existence, called "salvation" in Christianity. Secondly, a belief system is organized around five basic questions, the answers to which give form to the unsatisfactory nature of present experience. The formulation is shared by the members of the culture or religion whose views the belief system organizes and expresses. To be a "member" is to accept or hold exactly those beliefs organized in that way. The five basic beliefs constituting a belief system are the following:

1. Shared views of *what* is unsatisfactory about present experience.
2. Shared views about the source of that unsatisfactory situation.
3. Shared views of the nature of the delivering force through which the *source* of evil is defeated.

4. Shared views of what a resolved situation would look like.
5. Shared views of the "Way," or the path to follow, to this perfection, if such a catechism is necessary.

Let us look, now, to these beliefs in the American cultural religion.

1 and 2. *The Nature and Source of the Problem (Evil).* The problem that makes the present unsatisfactory is a break in meaningful social relations, or the inability to maintain a satisfying social institution. The threatened unit is usually the family or its larger counterparts, community, and nation. There are several regular sources of this threat. For instance, the members of a family may be beset by extramarital sex, honky-tonks, or bad companions, or overwhelmed by disease or an unscrupulous landlord. Communities are disrupted by interlopers, criminal elements who take what they want by force, rather than abiding by the standards of "law and order." They are unattached (and therefore uncivilized) males, ruthless, unprincipled representatives of non-family social institutions who rip off the little person (examples might be bankers, industrialists, syndicate criminals). Nations are threatened by foreign armies and alien ideologies. However diverse, all these sources have one thing in common: they are all external to the community, or to the group within the community that they attack. The television reviewer for *The New York Times,* known as "Cyclops," has put this eloquently:

It used to be that God was the detective, whether or not He chose to explain His mysterious ways; and what we couldn't bear to blame on God, we gave to the Devil as his due. Along came the Enlightenment, the idea of progress and the perfectibility of man, and then 19th-century science. We were going to fix things up, and ourselves. Alas, it seems not to have worked out satisfactorily. Without God or the Devil to take the rap, we have only ourselves to blame. That burden is insupportable and so we desperately look elsewhere—psychic energy within, deep space without, invisible demons, spooks, nameless evil. What on television used to be blamed on either the Cold War or the Mafia . . . now appears inexplicable except in terms of the malign workings of the parapsychologist beyond. . . . That way nobody is guilty.[1]

The people who are having the problem are not themselves responsible for it. They are, in a word, innocent and hence basically good. They may be impotent or afraid, but they are guilty of nothing more. Their deliverance frees them to live not a transformed life, but the naturally good life they would have lived had nothing previously intervened. From the height of the classic drama to the anti-Western of today, the externality of evil remains a consistent characteristic of the American belief system.

3. *The Source of the Good: Who Will Deliver Us from Evil?* If the townspeople are impotent or afraid, yet sorely troubled, who will deliver them? The predominance of American cultural faith is in the individual messiah. Where all institutions fail, from the police to the Catholic Church, the individual will succeed. Not just any individual, but one whose individuality combines the essentially human with some special power source unavailable to ordinary humans. This special

power is not superhuman or supernatural, but some especially desired human ability honed to razor-sharp efficiency. More often than not, this special ability— whether a quick draw, iron fists, or kung-fu physical agility—will be combined with an almost uncanny coolness and imperturbable self-control in the face of evil incarnate. In any case, it will always be necessary for the individual hero to dispatch the villain with an act of violence. This is justified by the righteousness of the cause and the combined inability of the official representatives of law and order and the unrecalcitrant stubbornness of the evil one (who always draws first). This individual deliverer in the ritual drama has a mysterious past, is unmarried and therefore "free" to come and go at will, and invariably male. Finally, the individual's deliverance of the community is a self-sacrificing deed. Either *he* dies, or his way of life dies. Who needs a fast gun when no one else carries a weapon?

4. *To What Are We Delivered?* The situation into which we are delivered in the classic form is family and the family-community, stabilized and promoted by schools and churches, by law and order, by peace, tranquillity, and domesticity. Women make it possible. Their strength and centrality in family life is the mark of civilization. The adolescent irresponsibility of men makes deliverance necessary. The responsible life is married family life. Behind the gun is a man; behind the man is a woman. She gives the whole enterprise merit and purpose.

5. *The Way.* Within the ritual drama itself, there is little room for instruction in the "Way" toward future

dreams from present problems. Such things are unnecessary when the battle is eschatological, the final
heroic encounter, the decisive victory. Nevertheless,
though the battle be won for the community, the sober
day-to-day task of realizing what is possible through
membership in the community is still with us. Popular
magazines are our manuals of catechism; and they generally equate fulfillment with certain physical appearances, and with a breadth of social graces and *savoir-
faire.* But we learn such things in weekly and monthly
installments, and not by ritual drama.

There is one exception to this generalization concerning the Way. There is another strong belief system
in American culture. This secondary system exists in
conjunction with the dominant system, rather than in
competition with it. Where the dominant system pictures salvation as some form of community, this secondary system focuses upon a particular image of humanity
as the fulfillment of the individual. The fulfilled individual is able to control *social* situations through mental
and physical preparedness. The same films that show us
the way in which Bogart or Wayne or Eastwood delivers us from evil also show us a hero who is totally self-
contained and able to handle every conceivable social
situation. When we participate in this secondary system, the Way does involve our attendance at ritual
drama, and our attachment to every detail of the lives
and careers of these "stars" in fan magazines and gossip
columns as well as on the screen. A successful parody on
our attachment to this secondary belief system is
Woody Allen's *Play It Again, Sam,* which begins with
Woody at a showing of *Casablanca* studying Bogart,
and in which a regularly appearing Bogart-image in-

structs Woody in his conquest of the female of the species.

THE WORSHIP CEREMONIES OF THE AMERICAN CULTURAL RELIGION: POPULAR CULTURE GENRES

Any unit of popular culture succeeds in its ritual function when it affirms the dominant cultural belief system. The same is true of popular culture media themselves. They are not all equally effective, at least not in the same ways. Television is the medium best able to perform the function of ritual confirmation. Films present a distinctively different type of ritual confirmation. In some ways films are more epic, classic, and belief-determining by virtue of their ability to combine the verbal articulation of particular beliefs with specific images. Films, however, are not so *effective* ritualistically as television. Still less effective—though no less comprehensive in scope—are popular magazines, certain types of literature (for example, detective fiction, science fiction, Gothic romances), country music, and professional sports.

Television. Like film, television generally assumes a dramatic form, but it is more effective than film in presenting belief-system ritual. Television has two distinct advantages over films. First, it combines formula format (the same thing happens every week) with preestablished time slot (at the same time every week). This is like the eleven o'clock Sunday morning worship services—knowing where and when we are supposed to worship, we show up prepared. Anticipation of the experience brings a preparedness which makes us all the more open to worship. We not only desire a certain experience in worship, but time-slot scheduling practically guarantees that we will get what we want. Similarly, when we sit down to watch *Marcus Welby,* we fully anticipate that another person, shattered by inexplicable and irremediable disease, will be helped to face this tragedy with dignity and courage. When Dr. Welby accomplishes another "cure," we come away believers once again. The second advantage of TV over film is its ability to establish constancy of character, elevating representative messianic roles to mythological proportions without straining credibility. The Lone Ranger and Superman strain credibility by making the power by which they deliver too overt or too supra-natural. Marcus Welby, Columbo, Kojak, and John Walton raise more universally human traits to quasi-divine sources of redeeming power. Do we fret that Perry Mason never loses a case? Hardly. If he did, we would stop watching.

Films. Films attempt the same apotheosis of character by combining the Hollywood star system with the genre film (as, for example, John Wayne Westerns). But films can match neither the patterned formula of television shows nor the time-slot regularity of their presentation. On the other hand, films have the advantage of giant visual images, an audience gathered outside the home, and the ability to create more convincingly the impression of eschatological urgency. A film is a one-time experience; further adventures will not be forthcoming next week. In such a setting, all the elements of the confrontation of good and evil swell to immense significance. An auditorium or arena outside the home, with groups of strangers drawn together to share this one experience, is the setting for both the movies and professional sports. The difference in professional sports is the preestablished camaraderie of the "fan." In the viewing of films it is the film alone that unites its audience—except on those rare occasions when Bogart buffs gather to watch *Casablanca* or *Across the Pacific.* But even the shared viewing experience is important in measuring the effectiveness of television and films. We often watch television by ourselves, in our own homes, on console screens whose images we can turn off or on, and to which we can add more red or green as suits our preference. Television-watching is more personal. But the film experience may be more powerful ritualistically because we come together with others for it. We receive contextual group support. What we expect and our responses to it are validated by like responses of those around us. Laughing or weeping in your own living room is one thing; laughing and weeping along with three hundred others is quite another. All that we experience is reinforced because others experience the same, and at the same time. We are joined to them; we rise out of our lonely selves and share our basic emotions. This is the power of worship in a congregational setting. In addition, the film-viewing experience has as much advantage over watching television as a Billy Graham rally has over weekly worship in your local church. Watching television is routine; going to the movies is special. When we go to the movies or to a Billy Graham rally, we know it is a one-time thing. We hope for an experience that will be full and complete and final in one evening.

Popular Magazines. Although they feature present problems and their sources, and tantalize with pictures of some of the already-saved brothers and sisters, popular magazines are less concerned with immediate resolution, and therefore are less urgent in their appeal. They are, in fact, instructional manuals in the Way to salvation. They assume that though the problem has been examined and its source identified, much is left for the communicant to complete.

Country Music. Country music is effective by the ritual simplicity of its consistent thematic organization of life's problems around a family/housewife/mother motif or a country-city dialectic. Undergirding the power of the repeated ritual themes represented in country music is a glamourous star system, reminiscent of Hollywood in the '40s. Unlike Hollywood stars, however, country-music performers spend much of the year in plush, bedroomed buses, touring the county fairs and backwoods towns of the Southern and Midwestern United States. They appear as melodic theophanies for the working people whose hard-earned money has made millionaires of more than twenty-five of these superstars.

Genre Literature. Popular literature includes the fiction best sellers, Gothic romances, science fiction, and detective fiction. These obviously all involve story, and so can communicate all the tension and urgency in their resolutions that eschatological ritual demands. But genre literature cannot match the staying power of the word-image combinations of television, film, and popular magazines. We may get excitedly carried away in the concluding chapters, when the resources of good finally triumph over evil, but much of this must take place within our imaginations. In television and films the actors and actresses, though only acting the parts, are absolutely and undeniably *outside* our minds.

Nevertheless, genre literature provides a functioning "worship ceremony" within the American belief system, and an effective one. In this study we will examine only detective fiction. It is especially important for the way in which it presents an urbanized version of the Western form which has much of the anti-Western about it. The significance of this comment will become more clear after Chapters 2 and 3.

So, we are ready to begin. Chapters 2 and 3 will introduce the major categories for our analysis. As we learn these, we will be doing belief-systems analysis of one of the worship ceremonies—popular films. Chapter 4 examines country music. It asserts that the family in the American belief system, and an analysis of the problems of life as threats to the family, is the key to understanding this kind of music. Themes of city versus country, the truck driver as popular hero, and the social protest of Tom T. Hall are discussed as well. Chapter 5 treats the images of male and female proffered by popular magazines, where what we will call the subdominant American belief system is operative. Chapter 6 analyzes the developing concept of the family in television—in situation comedies, soap operas, and *The Waltons.* Chapter 7 approaches an analysis of detec*tive* fiction, as differentiated from detec*ting* fiction, especially in the best-selling Travis McGee Series by John D. MacDonald. Finally, Chapter 8 will sum up, draw conclusions, and give specific recommendations concerning the significance of American cultural religion for the active life of the church.

2

Films:

THE CLASSIC WESTERN—
RITUAL AFFIRMATION OF POPULAR
CULTURE

What do George Wallace, Ralph Nader, Humphrey Bogart, and John Wayne have in common? They are all typically American Western heroes, of course, although you may not have thought so.

We are a people raised on quick draws and shoot-outs, on six-guns, cattle drives, and swinging doors. We can spot the obvious difference between dance-hall girls and schoolmarms, the white-hatted sheriffs and black-garbed gunslingers. Our introduction to classical music was the *William Tell* Overture in *The Lone Ranger.* The elemental outline of the Western is more familiar to us than our own biography.

But familiarity has bred a contemptuously casual attitude toward the Western's cultural significance in American life. That which we know so well, we don't really know at all. The Western is the classic ritual form, the "High Mass," of the predominant American belief system. This may explain why it is not more appreciated. The average Christian lay person has been through the Sunday morning worship service hundreds of times, but just ask him or her to describe in detail the parts of the order of worship. Though we know the Western, we don't know the order of its parts. Wallace,

Nader, Bogart, and Wayne share a ritual function in the "High Mass" of the American belief system. It is time to pay attention, and the only place to begin is where it all first came together, the Western.

The term "Western" does not necessarily mean "cowboy" movies, or films dealing with the American West between 1870 and 1910. The structural elements of the typical American Western may be found in films set in other periods, and employing various possible contents. This will become obvious when we compare two classic expressions of the genre: *Casablanca,* set in North Africa in World War II, and *Shane.* The former is a Western in form only, while the latter is a Western in both form and content.

THE CLASSIC WESTERN FORM[2]

The Setting

The most significant element in the Western form, and certainly the one without which the Western could never perform its ritual function, is the setting. The Western is set at the edge of the conflict of civilization and savagery, of advancing progress and rampant barbarianism. Settled social life, represented by family, church, and school, is never the problem in the classic Western—it is the chief value, for the sake of which all is done. The problem is the threatened breakup of the community. The community under threat is not just any community. The Western represents for Americans that historical time in which all that America stands for was finally and successfully accomplished. The last internal squabbles of youth were settled, out of which emerged a mature, responsible, law-abiding nation.

The "frontier" in the Western is the outpost of progressive civilization. Here the untamed, often savage wilderness makes its stand against the forces of law and order, who fight for the farmer, the schoolmarm, and the future of us all. Significantly, we do not doubt the outcome.[3] We do not fear that civilization will lose and savagery win. We already know the outcome; it is part of our self-understanding as Americans. The victory of the hero over the villain is not, then, a surprise or a great unexpected joy for us. It is the reaffirmation of what we believe as Americans should happen, and therefore must always happen. It is the ritually repeated drama of how it was that we seized the moment, defeated the enemy, and became who we are today. In ritual drama, the last *frontier* becomes the *last* frontier, in the "eschatological" sense, and thus becomes definitive for American self-understanding. Eschatology in Christian theology is the study of the "Last Day," the "day" upon which all human trials and troubles are finally and fully resolved. In an eschatological setting, all sin and evil come to an end, and salvation begins. Therefore any film claiming to be a Western, in the classic sense, must have the eschatological setting. Any film not explicitly a Western whose setting is American and eschatological may be essentially a Western.

The Nature of Its Adversaries

The adversaries in the Western form are simplistically good and evil foes. In the classic Western form, no characters participate in both good and evil. The delivering-hero figure is clearly good. He[4] is morally pure, restrained in his behavior in a socially acceptable way, mannered (he eats with a fork and tips his hat to the ladies), clean, and respectful of social institutions and ritual. He has style and integrity. He draws only when drawn upon, and would *never* shoot anyone in the back. The villain, on the other hand, is the personification of evil, either in a chilling, mythical style of his own, or in a way that flaunts the very social conventions he threatens. The former type displays a surface demeanor of steely contempt, masking a perverse and sadistic cruelty, an unending depth of heartlessness. The other type looks uncouth and acts it. He has slovenly eating habits; he treats women roughly. He has a dirty, unshaven face, accompanied by a long scar and missing or blackened teeth. He is noisy and shows a snarling disrespect for decent people and their institutions. He is given to outbursts of wanton, destructive violence as vengeance or as joke. The opponents that square off in the Eschaton are the embodiment of good and evil, Christ and Antichrist, respectively. So, in the Western, the hero and the townspeople he defends are good, while the villain is clearly and simplistically evil.

No one ever promised a peaceful apocalypse. The very term "apocalypse" adds the violent retribution we wish upon the source of the evil crushing our lives. An eschaton is basically a time of transition, the last days of the old age and the first of the new. Few of us have sufficient grace to wish our enemies well in the transition. Since they are recalcitrant to the end, we have no other choice but to violently annihilate them. So it is with the Western—there is always a violent ending. The hero would not choose the course to which he is forced—he is basically a man of peaceful ways. But we all know what must be done, and much of the film prepares us to accept the inevitability of that which we wanted all along, the destruction of the villain, the clear, clean victory of the forces of good.[5]

We can now state one of the most consistent principles of the American belief system: the source of evil is always external to those suffering the effects of evil.

Justifiable Homicide

Although the ending of the Western is inevitably violent, this must occur within accepted American standards of law and order. Dispatching the villain must be an act for which the hero is not accountable in court. To arrest the hero for depriving the villain of his civil rights would scandalize us. We would simply not accept it.

That the ritual setting of the Western is eschatological contributes to our willingness to let the hero's violent activity go unquestioned. The hero delivers us *from* evil itself, *to* a satisfying and fulfilled life. The policeman who shoots the rapist-murderer without sufficient warning does not have the eschatological context to justify him, though as an American with a gun he may identify momentarily with the image of the Western deliverer-hero. But life goes on where we live it, and this policeman may be suspended for his act. In the Western, however, the story ends when *the* villain (or villains) is destroyed; we do not feel that more are lurking in the shadows. Evil has been annihilated; the good life has been preserved, or established.

The hero must act either as the law or because the particular individuals holding that responsibility are unable to perform their duty. Either he puts on the badge before he goes out for the gunfight, or he goes to meet the villain because the sheriff cannot or will not act. John Ford's cynicism is showing when he casts Andy Devine as the sheriff in *The Man Who Shot Liberty Valance:* we aren't five minutes into the film before we know he will be unable to face Lee Marvin in the final scenes. When Spencer Tracy visits the sheriff's office in *Bad Day at Black Rock,* he finds the bleary-eyed sheriff sleeping off a hangover in one of his own cells! In *Death Wish,* the film's premise is that the police will be ineffective against the mugger-rapist fiend of the city. One scene contrasts the evasive action of a subway cop who moves into another car when he sees the mugger types approaching, with the repose of vigilante Charles Bronson who sits calmly reading his newspaper, pearl-handled .32 six-shooter tucked inside his coat, silently awaiting the unsuspecting muggers. There are, of course, many Westerns in which the protagonist already is, or soon becomes, the sheriff. In any case, justice must be served—legally.

The Characters of the Western Drama [6]

The Townspeople

There are primarily four different kinds of townspeople in the Western form: women, inheritors of the torch, sidekicks and supporting characters, and corrupt politicians and bureaucrats. With the exception of the last-mentioned, all are basically good.

"The most important single fact about the group of townspeople is that there are women in it." [7] This point cannot be overemphasized. The hero and the villains are always male. This is partly because of the male chauvinism of many Americans, and partly because such roles depend upon the stylized look of physical power and the possibility of rash and immature expressions of violence—behavior deemed unworthy of women. Women are the strong, ongoing, stable influences in a social order. Their concern is family, community, schools, church, law and order. The woman is for the civilized way of handling disputes, and against violence. The most famous example of this may be Grace Kelly's role as the Quaker bride in *High Noon.*

Women represent civilization, and so they belong with the townspeople. They are the domesticators of men. They take a man running free and wild and turn him into a responsible (and tame) member of the community. Every man knows that a woman ties you down. There are some ambiguous features[8] represented in this symbolic role of the woman, but generally she plays a role steeped in the positive values of the established community. Often she is the fulcrum of the plot situation, as when she is a widow whose ranch is being foreclosed or a schoolmarm threatened by vicious outlaws. In the latter case, there are obviously sexual undertones: will the pure and honest woman we wish to mother our children be defiled by savages, whose perverse potency is part of their mythical style? The fear is with us, from the terror evoked when the beautiful, blond Dale Arden is menaced by vile Oriental potentates and obese winged hawk-men in *Flash Gordon,* to the surprise and relief elicited in the spoof of this anxiety in the first meeting of Robert Redford and Katharine Ross in *Butch Cassidy and the Sundance Kid.* Normally the sexual threat to the woman is not nearly so significant as the threat to her place in the future of civilization and its stable, peaceful communities.

Two kinds of women belong to the Western form. We have been talking about the townswomen of positive value: the schoolmarm, the rancher's daughter, the farmer's wife. But there is another woman in the town, a woman of dubious value and of established moral turpitude. She is the fallen woman, the woman of easy virtue, the dance-hall girl. Her love is free. She never expects the hero or the villain to marry her the "morning after." Her very presence disarms the primal sexual anxiety in most Westerns, since she is available to release pent-up sexual drives and tensions. She may be the slapped-around floozy whose love for the villain is as certain a death wish as any can be. Or her love for the hero, though destined never to be satisfied, may get her shot by mistake in the final scenes—applying the ultimate irony by having her die "in his arms." Her dress and her language are loose and suggestive, particularly compared with the high-necked frilly blouse and schoolbook diction of the other type of woman. Often her name is Frenchy, or Chihuahua, or Dallas—reminiscent of erotic, exotic, or "wide open" towns—while her antithesis is called Lucy Mallory or Clementine Carter. Normally this woman is never allowed to marry the hero, even when they have yearned after each other for twenty years, as with *Gunsmoke*'s famous duo, Matt Dillon and Miss Kitty.

A secondary function of the redeemer-hero has been to save this poor fallen woman from her past, or at least provide the occasion in which her true goodness emerges. So, in John Ford's classic 1939 film, *Stagecoach*, Claire Trevor gets to marry John Wayne; and in

Walking Tall, Buford sends his B-girl informer off on the bus with the words, "All the charges against you have been taken off the books."

What are inheritors of the torch? As we shall see, the hero is part town, part wilderness, part settled, part restless and free. He combines the best characteristics of both, like a Christ-figure. He can maintain this ambiguous mixture only until he has resolved the problems confronting the townspeople. Then he must choose either marriage and membership in the community with its concomitant responsibilities, or the free wandering but lonely life, and moving on. Most of the time he moves on. Who will carry on? There is often a prominent male townsperson who supports the hero and then assumes the leadership of the saved, new community. He is the one to whom the hero passes the torch. He is almost always a professional person, or does some job upon which the future of civilization depends. He may merely represent the community in receiving the torch, as Walter Brennan does when receiving the Japanese-American boy's war medal from Spencer Tracy at the end of *Bad Day at Black Rock.* Or he may himself be the future leader of the new community, as the lawyer Ransom Stoddard (Jimmy Stewart) becomes after he acquires a reputation for having killed notorious outlaw Liberty Valance—actually shot down by Tom Doniphon (played, of course, by John Wayne). Though John Ford intended a cynical lament of the unjust passing of the Western hero, *The Man Who Shot Liberty Valance* still represents an excellent example of the inheritor-of-the-torch role in the Western. Stoddard is more than just one of the townspeople; he is the civilized side (domesticated and sissified, Ford would say) of Doniphon. He is the best of the hero-deliverer remaining behind—the best, that is, for the civilized world of family, community, church, and government.

Women and torch-inheritors are supporting characters. Two additional types are worth mentioning. First, there are characters, often professionals (lawyers, newspaper editors, doctors), who support the hero and are often the precipitating cause of the hero's action (for instance, they may get beaten up by the bad guys). They are from the East, and are failures at self-respect and success, though skilled at their jobs. They have come West to get away from the failure they inevitably bring with them—the people of the West aren't so choosy. Often they are superficially cowards, and alcoholics. Though educated, literate, and vested with the future of civilization, they are no match for the villain. Part of the plot in John Ford's *Stagecoach* deals with whether or not the alcoholic doctor played by Thomas Mitchell can be sobered up in time to deliver the baby of the cavalry officer's wife. (Mitchell not only sobered up, he won the Academy Award for doing so!)

The second type are sidekicks. These are not always townspeople, as with Tonto, for instance. In fact, they are quite often members of ethnic or racial minority groups, and therefore marginal townspeople at best, in the classic Western form. They are easily identified as traveling with the hero, though in an obviously subservient role. Part of the shame at this country's treatment of nonwhite Americans is clearly unavoidable in the sidekick phenomenon. Although sidekicks are not always nonwhite, as they are with the Lone Ranger and his "faithful Indian companion" and the Green Hornet's Oriental assistant Cato, they continue to represent dominant/subservient male relations; for example, adult-child (Batman and Robin) or adult-old man (Roy Rogers and Gabby Hayes). Or they may combine many of these together, as in *Mannix,* where a white male boss is assisted by a black female secretary! Some sidekicks are picked upon and humiliated by the villain, while others—such as those played by actor Woody Strode—project such images of fierce power as to discourage any tampering with the merchandise. Villains often have members of their gangs that play a somewhat similar sidekick relationship to the chief villain, the major difference being that while the hero treats his sidekick like a human being, the villain is always slapping and berating his sidekick for incompetency.

Finally, there are within the town persons who represent all that we recognize as wrong with civilization. These are bureaucrats, politicians, corrupt bankers, land scalpers, traders who sell guns to the Indians, and baronial railroaders. They may be the villains, or they may turn the townspeople against the hero, inhibiting his ability to deal forthrightly with the villain. They are slick, oily, dressed like fops, all smiles and sly deals. And they are as ruthless and cruel as any savage outlaw. Sometimes they "own" the town as does Posenor in *Billy Jack,* and Regan in *Bad Day at Black Rock.* No more visually exciting cinematic casting of this type of townsperson exists than that in Sergio Leone's *Once Upon a Time in the West.* The two main villains are Morton, the railroad entrepreneur, whose inner perversity of soul is mirrored in the tubercular bone illness progressively crippling his body and confining him to his railroad car; and his chief assistant, Frank, played by Henry Fonda, whose quiet manner and pale blue eyes mask a cold and venomous heart, delighting in torture and unmoved by the murder of children.

The Villains

The single most important fact about the villain in the Western form is that he is the source of the evil situation besetting the town. The townspeople are, with the exception of corrupt bureaucrats and bankers, essentially good. The evil threatening them is not something that Sunday school or psychoanalysis will correct—its source is external to those who suffer its consequences. The evil situation is not peripheral or incidental—it is a direct impediment to the realization of everything for which the town was founded and toward which its future is directed. "Salvation" in the Western form is civilization, defined as family, community, school, church, successful business, free press, and law and order. The villain is the source of evil because he threatens to derail the salvation express.

The most interesting fact about the villain is the ambiguity of his role in the Western form. Civilization is a two-sided idea. Though all the values of civilization are admirable and generally desirable, they are neither fully satisfying nor free. We must give up something else to acquire them, and when what we have won turns sour on us, we begin to wonder whether the price was too high. We identify with the gangster in films because he cuts himself loose from proper social behavior, and with unrelenting violence asserts himself and rises to wealth and power, defeating the city, the successor to civilization and our dominator.[9] The Western villain or savage evokes the same ambiguous feelings in us.

The presence of both noble and diabolical manifestations of savagery reflects the same kind of ambiguity about the progress of civilization. . . . The savage symbolizes the violence, brutality, and ignorance which civilized society seeks to control and eliminate, but he also commonly stands for certain positive values which are restricted or destroyed by advancing civilization: the freedom and spontaneity of wilderness life, the sense of personal honor and individual mastery, and the deep camaraderie of men untrammelled by domestic ties. In both roles it turns out that the savage must be destroyed, but in one case we rejoice and in the other feel nostalgically sorry.[10]

The Hero-Deliverer

The Western hero assumes two roles in the Western form. Primarily he resolves the conflict between the savage villain and the townspeople by destroying the villain. Secondarily, he represents in his person the best elements of the villain combined with some of the best elements of the townspeople. The elements of the villain in the hero are attractive qualities, and appreciated as such by the townspeople as long as the hero is the means by which the source of evil can be destroyed. Ultimately, however, after the villain has been destroyed, the townspeople reject these qualities, because they represent an alternative life-style to that espoused by the town. To be unmarried, free to roam and ramble from town to town, to frequent bars and poker tables, to be fast with a gun and rough with his fists—all these character traits are desirable in the man who will have to face the villain. But they are only the source of more trouble, and a temptation to the married menfolk, once law and order have been established. Unlike the villain, the hero is respectful of the family and the church, polite to the ladies, believes in the importance of school, and basically is a man of honor and integrity. The Western is about the resolution of the conflict between good and evil. But it may also focus on the internal tensions of a man bearing two conflicting life-styles within himself. So it makes the hero's act of deliverance a tragic self-sacrifice. When this tragedy becomes central to a Western, the classic form can only be maintained by a strong justification of the act of sacrifice. When the justification is lacking, we have what we will discuss in the next chapter, the anti-Western.

The Western hero is not only the source of good through his resolution of the conflict between townspeople and savage, and thus the deliverer; but he is also salvation itself. He is the embodiment of a certain image of humanity, the fulfillment of a vision of human perfection within the community context. But this perfection is an individual one, and herein lie the roots of conflict within the community.

When the community itself is threatened, the hostile assault of a common enemy makes individual differences seem petty. However, once the external threat to the community has been defeated, the normal conflicting claims of individuals to the few positions of place, power, and wealth in a society become all-important. Members of the society are faced with the task of establishing and maintaining their individual identities, while the society attempts to restrict nonconforming individuals, reducing as much eccentricity as possible to manageable, socially acceptable types of behavior. This is a different source of evil to human life from that which threatens the community as a whole. The source of evil here is the community itself, at least those aspects of the community which require that individual expression bow to institutionalized social aims.

Is there a style of individual behavior to which we can conform and still maintain our sanity? For Christians the normative statement of full humanity is Jesus Christ. For Americans the normative ritual expression of realized human fulfillment is the Western hero. We identify with this hero-deliverer in the Western formula not because he is the deliverer of the community, but because of the style and image of humanity he projects. We will call it, taking the word in its popular sense, "sophistication."

Sophistication is the quality of being not only at home in every possible situation, but in control. Such control necessitates extensive knowledge of one's environment, mastery of physical skills of self-defense, and tremendous self-confidence. In the Western, this may involve an ability to live in harmony with the natural wilderness, a keen sense of good and evil in people, a wariness which makes it impossible for cheaters to get the upper hand. The ability to shoot quick and true is tempered by the "cool" sense to resist calling upon gun or fists except when absolutely necessary. There may be variations, adapting to the variations in the story line. Nevertheless, the form calls for the hero to evidence inner strength and self-confidence in any and all situations, a sophistication unshaken by whatever turn of events.

We all identify with the image of the sophisticated, self-contained hero. He is, in fact, a hero not only because he delivers us, but also because he is what we would like to be. He is the incarnate fulfillment of the dream we dream for our own individuality. In the Western form, this inner self-mastery is manifest in a number of typical ways. The Western hero lives by a code of honor, not to some intrinsic standard, but to himself, to what he must be. He does what he has to do. He is the fully realized, imperturbable, socially invulnerable individual.

In addition to the "code" which seems to guide his actions, the hero is *"par excellence* a man of leisure."[11] He is not grubbily anxious about tomorrow, like the rest of us. He never seems to be gainfully employed. Like the lilies of the field, he neither toils nor spins, but he always seems to be dressed to enhance a stylish image. Most of us are forever breaking out in cold sweat with the fear that unforeseen expenditures will tip a precariously balanced budget into an unmanageable burden of red-inked items. Not so the Western hero, whose day is always free for standing at the bar, playing poker, courting fair maidens. Even when the hero is employed, his job seems virtually free of drudgery and effort-expending physical labor.

Again, he is consistently the center of attention in every social group and gathering. He may indulge in some drinking, but he never gets drunk, relinquishing control. He never loses at poker, unless the plot calls for it. And, though he is kind and considerate in his actions toward bar girls and women of the night, he is not a woman chaser. He generally stands alone, and does not associate unnecessarily with any particular group. He is ready for anything. Clint Eastwood, in *High Plains Drifter,* surprises the three thugs in the barbershop with a gun carefully concealed but ready underneath the sheet covering him in the barber's chair. When

McCabe in *McCabe and Mrs. Miller* finishes the last of the company hoodlums with a small derringer nobody knew he had, we marvel joyously once again how "cool" these guys are. They know enough to be ready for anything.

The characteristic most representative of the controlled sophistication of the Western hero is "restraint." The Western hero never becomes emotionally aroused by the disrespectful taunts of the villain. He is never tricked into acting prematurely. A typical plot device in the Western form has the hero continually refusing to get involved in defending the townspeople or repeatedly ignoring slurs on his reputation. Only when the intolerable evil of the villain has gathered its forces to perform some monstrous act or to force the hero's hand in some final deck-stacked confrontation, does the hero act. Then he acts quickly, and with surprising flourish, to perform the violence which we clearly recognize as necessary to deliver us. But even then, the hero maintains self-control, he never attacks the villain until the villain has taken the first step to destroy the hero. We love it, even though we know full well that the real Wyatt Earp stole around through the alley and shot the villain in the back.

Two Classic Prototypes: *Casablanca* and *Shane*

George Stevens' *Shane*, a Western in both form and content, is set in the Western frontier. It is a 1953 movie, shot in a vast expanse of beautiful landscapes upon which a small town huddles, a few ramshackle buildings all on the same side of the same muddy street. So bare is the settler's grip upon the Western wilderness that the land seems almost forbidding in its enormity. The visual simplicity of the setting so contributes to the mythical style and feeling of the film that everything "seems to be happening at the bottom of a clear lake."[12] The ranchers are the source of evil initially, since they need a free and open range for grazing cattle. The homesteading farmers who have come to settle and tame the land (fencing it in) play the part of the innocent townspeople. The ranchers try to terrorize the farmers into leaving the area, a task doomed ultimately to failure, since we know that the land was eventually settled and civilized.

Michael Curtiz' *Casablanca* is a Western only in form. It takes place supposedly at the time in which the film was made, 1942, in North Africa, in a neutral zone governed by Vichy France. To Casablanca come all those fleeing Nazi-occupied Europe and its totalitarian dictatorships. Casablanca is, therefore, the frontier, the meeting point of the free world and military Nazi enslavement. In Casablanca the forces of good (Western democracy and the free world) meet the forces of evil (Nazi domination), and the future of the whole world hangs in the balance. No setting could be more eschatological. Here also good and evil become incarnate in two men whose final confrontation will turn the tide to victory or defeat for civilization. In a tradition as old as war itself (as with David and Goliath, and Shakespeare's *Antony and Cleopatra*) each side "chooses" a man to fight for its cause and to determine the final result for both. As soon as we see that Third Reich Commander Strasser is played by Conrad Veidt and the American Rick by Humphrey Bogart, we know who will win this battle of wits and wiles. Correspondingly, we experi-

ence the same assurance in *Shane*, finding handsome
Alan Ladd cast in the title role and ugly Jack Palance as
the ranchers' evil hired gun. The point is that the victory we so appreciate and celebrate in both films is one
that reassures us deeply that all we believe is true and
honorable and will ultimately be vindicated. That
which should happen will happen.

In both *Casablanca* and *Shane*, good and evil are
simplistically portrayed. There is no ambiguity, certainly, in the characterizations of Bogart and Ladd as
heroes, or in the roles of Veidt and Palance as villains.
Even today, to be an American in *Casablanca* is decid-
edly better than being a Nazi. Veidt's Strasser is a more
mature example of the villain in the Western form,
closer to the corrupt banker or politician townsperson
than to the animalistic Liberty Valance played with
gross glee by Lee Marvin in *The Man Who Shot Liberty
Valance*. Strasser is after all a man of education and
good upbringing, mannered, restrained—everything
that we fear in the slick, sanitized surface beauty of
heartless modern technology and its representatives.
But even on the more conscious level, to be a Nazi is as
unambiguously evil as any film villain can be. Palance
in *Shane* achieves something of the same effect by housing the self-mastery of the hero in black, silver-studded
clothes, behind beady eyes and a teeth-flashing, sardonic smile.

In *Shane*, we know that a shoot-out will occur between Ladd and Palance, even though Shane does not
want to get involved. He resists the inevitable until he
either must fight or allow Van Heflin as the farmer to
be killed. Shane's act is forced upon him, inevitably so,
and we know it will be violent. In *Casablanca*, we sense

that a final confrontation between Bogart and Veidt may take place, but we are not sure that it will be violent. As surely and as justifiably as Ladd draws his gun and kills Palance to save Heflin and the future farmers of America, so Bogart draws his gun from his trench coat pocket and murders Veidt, not only to assure the escape of freedom fighter Henreid and Ingrid Bergman, but because Veidt draws his gun to shoot Bogart. Both Palance and Veidt draw first. That a movie about Germans and Americans in World War II should end in a classic Western quick-draw shoot-out is testimony to the enduring impact and significance of the traditional elements of the form.

Both homicides are justified not only by self-defense, and the justice of the cause, but by the inability of the forces of law and order effectively to dispatch the forces of evil. The action in *Shane* is far removed from judge, jury, and the efficient law enforcement operations of the East. And the ranchers control what local law is available. Shane must act because no one else will. The law in *Casablanca* is played with style and humor by Claude Rains, whose character is forced into a permissive attitude toward the Germans by his government's "neutrality." Though he constantly needles the German commander, Rains always says to Bogart, "I am powerless." When Rains is redeemed by Bogart's killing of Strasser, he drops a bottle of vichy water into a wastebasket, kicks the basket, and walks off into the fog of "darkest Africa" with Bogart to the closing words of the film (which Rains delivers): "This could be the beginning of a beautiful friendship." Not only is Bogart's action justified by the political handcuffs on Rains, but law and order is itself won over and redeemed!

There is no woman of dubious moral standing in *Shane,* and only a minor, but significant, one in *Casablanca.* But both films make up for this by assigning a major role to the schoolmarm, woman-of-virtue type. Jean Arthur as farmer Heflin's wife in *Shane* turns in a fine acting performance, recalling the warmth and inner beauty that Claire Trevor brought to the role of Dallas in *Stagecoach.* Typically, Arthur is against guns and violence, and—bringing us all to the edge of our seats—she falls in love with Shane. It is a perfect love, because there isn't the slightest chance that it can ever be consummated. It must remain eternally idealized, unexpressed, locked in the hearts of both, for they have equally pressing callings: the future of the civilized community, and the honor, strength, and stability of the family. Shane could take her with him—we all know she would go. But he cannot. She has no place in his life, and she belongs with her family, giving it the support she owes all of us. By 1953 histrionics were not so appropriate as in 1943, when Bogart gave up Bergman to Paul Henreid and the future of Western civilization. The you-belong-with-him-and-his-work speech at the end of *Casablanca* is now famous. Woody Allen repeats it in *Play It Again, Sam.* Bogart, trench coat collar up, hands in pockets, sends the misty-eyed Ingrid Bergman off with her husband, while telling us all explicitly what Ladd and Arthur don't say directly in *Shane.* Of course much more of the plot is devoted to the Bogart-Bergman love story in *Casablanca.*

Because of *Casablanca*'s modern setting, Ingrid Bergman's Ilsa is permitted the luxury of already having had a love affair with the hero, something unthinkable in *Shane.* But her virtuous image is intact, because we learn she was under the impression that her free-dom-fighter husband had died in a concentration camp. The minute he returns and needs her, she leaves the man she really loves (Bogart) and returns loyally to serve and give her affection to the man she married out of hero worship when she was a starry-eyed, teen-age daughter of a farmer. Later, after meeting Bogart again, and realizing that she could never leave him again, she puts her fate in his hands—and his decision is true to the form of the Western hero.

The woman of dubious moral value in *Casablanca* (called Yvonne) does not have a large part, but every scene in which she is featured is important to the film. Initially, when we see her at the bar in the film's open-ing sequence in Rick's café, we recognize her type im-mediately. She is drinking a little too heavily, and she looks a bit like a floozy. Her first scenes function to establish Rick's character: she makes desperate ad-vances to Rick, which he rebuffs with one-line put-downs:

She: Rick, where were you last night?
Rick: I can't remember that far back.
She: Where will you be tonight?
Rick: I don't make plans that far ahead.

All the while he is coolly ignoring her presence, his attention turned toward café business receipts. But the real goodness hidden behind his mask of indifference is revealed when he sends his bartender to escort her home safely. Her reputation as practically anybody's girl is reinforced when she returns indignantly the next night in the company of German officers. Has she gone over to the enemy? Unthinkable. What will relieve our anxiety by assuring us that she is really a good person down deep, and is only dating these Germans in impetuous anger over the way Rick treats her? Sure enough, in the emotionally charged scene in which freedom fighter Henreid leads the band in "The Marseillaise" and when the singing of the French drowns out the German national anthem which the Nazis are singing, there is a close-up of Yvonne. Though she's been sitting with the Nazis, she stands proudly, tears streaming down her face, singing "The Marseillaise."

Farmer Van Heflin and freedom fighter Paul Henreid are as classically inheritor-of-the-torch figures as ever appeared in Western-form films. Both are proud, dedicated, honest men, respected by the hero-deliverer; both are the leaders of the community of tomorrow. Both are family men, with devoted wives. Yet neither is able effectively to destroy the source of evil responsible for their problems. The imminent destruction of each by the source of evil is cause for the final actions of the hero. Except for the hero's special ability to destroy the villain, both Heflin and Henreid are represented as equal to the hero in qualities revered by civilization.

Neither film has supporting characters of the first type mentioned in the analysis above, professionals fleeing former failure. But both films employ a version of the sidekick stereotype. In *Shane* the role is taken by the narrator of the story, the boy Joey, played by Brandon de Wilde. Children are a minority group in the Western form, anyway. Joey not only idolizes Shane, providing a context for Shane's justification of his use of violence, but he represents the possibility that Shane's image of fulfilled human self-mastery may also be passed on. In the belief system for which community is salvation, Heflin's farmer as the inheritor of the torch becomes our leader on the "Way." But for the belief system that focuses on the image of humanity in Shane as salvation, the "Way" is explicitly incorporated into the film in the catechism-instruction that Shane gives to Joey.

In *Casablanca,* the sidekick role is played in more typical fashion by someone of a nonwhite race, Dooley Wilson, a black singer–piano player, whose portrayal of Sam is one of the most famous screen roles ever. Besides carrying Rick's luggage and working for him in his café, Sam is obviously a close friend and companion, who feels for Rick's emotional crisis. He tries to get Rick to go away for a few days of fishing and drinking and forgetting, a suggestion Rick rejects not because it is implausible, but clearly out of the self-pity and bitterness in which he (Rick) is mired. Sam's independence of Rick is seen when Sam chooses to stay behind and work in the café, rather than to go on with Rick to a life that no longer includes Sam's music. From the vantage point of the 1970's, the implicit racism of Sam's yes-boss relationship to Rick stands out glaringly, inhibiting our complete acceptance of the character of Sam. But, with that exception, in no other American classic does the sidekick figure play such a thematically prominent role. Sam's song, "As Time Goes By," is *the* key to the unity and moving ritual message of the film. From that piano pours forth the melody that links Bogart and Bergman. It is the central affirmation of the classic ritual form: "It's still the same old story, A fight for love and glory, A case of do or die. . . . The fundamental things apply, As time goes by." Furthermore, hidden in Sam's piano are the letters of transit, which figure so prominently in the plot. They are the means by which Bogart will free the underground rebel, and thus continue the defense of the free world against the Nazi terror.

Corrupt townspeople and bureaucratic politicians are absent from both these films. The reason is fairly simple. They represent the negative side of civilization; when they appear, the seminal elements of the anti-Western are also present. In the classic American Western form, the townspeople are all good and the threat is from outside the community itself. To bring the source of evil within the community is to dim the vision, to crack the superstructure of the world we are gambling so much to win. The highest ritual expressions of the system contain as few elements as possible to obscure the prize for which we fight. So in *Casablanca,* in which rich characterizations of minor characters abound, even Peter Lorre and Sidney Greenstreet, connivers *par excellence,* are sweet and lovable compared to the Nazis.

The same conditions probably account for the lack of ambiguity in the villains, Veidt and Palance. Both are so completely unsympathetic and evil that we never feel sorry for them for a moment; nor do we envy their freedom or power or skills.

The heroes in these films, Rick and Shane, are both single, and have mysterious pasts. Even the Germans can't get a full dossier on Rick Blaine. Shane is skilled with a gun, Rick with wit (though he proves able to match the villain Strasser in the shoot-out). Both are reluctant to get involved, and do so only when it is the only course left. Neither is much of a drinker by habit. Both perform acts of charity and support of the townspeople: Shane helps the farmer dig up a tree stump; Rick fixes a gambling table to enable a young couple to win passports. Both are sacrificial figures, giving up the woman they care for and their livelihood to defeat the villain. Shane rides off into the countryside, wounded, perhaps to die. Bogart walks off into Africa, away from Casablanca and the café he has so successfully established.

Of the sophistication of Alan Ladd in *Shane* and Humphrey Bogart in *Casablanca* nothing really needs to be said: they define the hero image. Of Ladd in *Shane,* Warshow says:

The hero (Alan Ladd) is hardly a man at all, but something like the Spirit of the West, beautiful in fringed buckskins. He emerges mysteriously from the plains, breathing sweetness and a melancholy which is no longer simply the Westerner's natural response to experience but has taken on spirituality. . . . The choice of Alan Ladd to play the leading role is alone an indication of this film's tendency. . . . Ladd is a [n] . . . "aesthetic" object, with some of the "universality" of a piece of sculpture; his special quality is in his physical smoothness and serenity, unworldly and yet not innocent, but suggesting that no experience can really touch him. Stevens has tried to freeze the Western myth once and for all in the immobility of Alan Ladd's countenance.[13]

Of the great, widely revered Humphrey Bogart, in his most representative role, who can add one cubit?

3

Films:

THE ANTI-WESTERN—
SKEPTICS IN THE COMMUNITY
OF FAITH

Frank Serpico is hiding out in the Netherlands with his faithful companion, Alfie. Alfie is a sheep dog, the only remaining living being Serpico can trust. Like the classic Western hero, Serpico discovered a threat to the future of the community in which he believed, and marshaled his courage for an ultimate confrontation. Unfortunately for Serpico, the source of evil turned out to be one of the institutions responsible for preserving the cherished values of the community, the New York City Police Department. If the source of corruption had been a few "bad apples," the diligence of the Knapp Commission would have been an ample substitute for the classic main street shoot-out. But it was not. Serpico is in hiding because the errant thread he pulled began to unravel the whole sweater.

Serpico's exploits have recently been elevated to symbolic stature. But he is hardly the first citizen to question the vision of America as salvation. The experience of the great depression drove a few intellectuals to a brief flirtation with alternative ideologies. Had these been forgotten, the unifying power of the challenges of the forties might have sustained the vision a few years longer. But Senator Joseph McCarthy and his supporters saw the precarious condition of the vision of American self-understanding more clearly than many other Americans. Their paranoid fear of Communism became an obsession, extracting confessions and repentance from the few who had doubted a decade or so before. Ironically, the general revelation that there were dissenters in our midst terrified us less than the ferocity of the purge itself!

The self-doubt raised by McCarthyism in our own country never had a chance to dissipate. When Americans later awoke to the shame of racial inequality and the sense of its guilt, political leaders, black or white, bearing the promise of a renewal of the vision of America fell to assassins. Then a small Asian war infected our self-image like a cancer. Although America responded by doing what we had always done, it now left a bad taste. The more involved we got, the more unprincipled and evil our every act seemed to be. We sought as leader an idol of the secure fifties, one who promised "to bring us together" and to speak for the American "silent majority." But this "idol" and his team have been exposed as arrogant, self-serving elitists, as thoroughly and unrelentingly corrupt as the New York City Police Department's worst opportunitists. A shock almost beyond remedy has been delivered to what vestiges of pride and self-confidence we had.

The first signs of the anti-Western appeared in the early fifties. Its popularity has continued to rise through the late sixties and early seventies. What do we mean by the term "anti-Western"? How is it related to the Western form we have already studied? To these questions we will now turn our attention.

What is an "anti-Western"? Simply, it is any dramatic

presentation within popular culture that criticizes an
element or elements of the classic Western form. The
anti-Western contends that a particular belief in the
system represented in the Western form is untrue,
naïve, and/or self-serving. It misrepresents the facts of
life in these United States. To be anti-Western is to be
critical of a particularly popular view of the meaning of
American life. The growing popularity of the anti-Western film indicates an increasingly widespread disen-
chantment with the classic form of American self-
understanding as represented in the Western form.
Critics of America's self-image have always existed on
the periphery. But the popularity of the anti-Western
has evidenced restlessness and dissatisfaction in the
mainstream of Middle America.

A few general observations on the "anti-Western"
may be in order. First, the anti-Western is almost entirely negative. Hence, the prefix "anti" is appropriate.
The mood of the anti-Western is therefore often pessi-
mistic, despairing, and nihilistic. The creative side of
belief-system construction in American popular culture
is to be found in science fiction.

Secondly, while the dominant belief system comes
under attack in the anti-Western, the subdominant system focused in the style of the hero becomes propor-
tionately more important. As confidence in the American *community* as the content of salvation has
diminished, interest has turned toward the self-contained *individual* as representative of what the fulfilled
life must be like. *Casablanca* is less popular today for its
view of the free, Western community than for the complete, Humphrey Bogart style of person it presents. It
is hardly coincidence that *Playboy* magazine, a cleverly

packaged do-it-yourself manual for attaining individual male fulfillment, began in the early fifties with the anti-Western and paralleled its growth and popularity.[14]

Our final general remark concerning the anti-Western is a confession. The line distinguishing Western from anti-Western is often a fine one. Many films may be both Western and anti-Western, employing traditional affirmations of some essential elements of the classic form in combination with critical rejection of others. The use of the category of anti-Western may be arbitrary—indeed, necessarily arbitrary. When do the first real anti-Westerns appear? At what point are the presence of anti-Western elements sufficient to qualify a film as anti-Western, rather than Western? You may notice in the following that such questions are not directly answered. In the films we will discuss we hope to make the term "anti-Western" a useful category in coming to grips with changing patterns in systems of belief in American culture. This is our only intention.

"EVIL" WITHIN THE "GOOD" COMMUNITY

Do you remember when the phrase "adult Western" came into vogue? The film was *High Noon* (1952). The story was of a marshal (Gary Cooper) who is retiring from law enforcement (symbolically represented by his marriage to a nonviolent Quaker played by Grace Kelly). The plot deals with Cooper's last task as marshal: he must delay his departure to confront three revenge-minded outlaws who are returning from the prison to which he sent them.

Why was *High Noon* called an "adult Western"? Did it deal more realistically with adult life or everyday events? Did it raise the formula film to the level of art? It did neither. While it is basically a traditional Western, *High Noon* faces openly some nagging suspicions that the classic American vision is flawed. This departure from the classic form was interpreted as an evidence of maturity, and earned it the label of "adult." The impotence of the townspeople has always been essential in justifying the violent act of the solitary hero in annihilating the villain. But *High Noon* dwells embarrassingly on Cooper's attempt to solicit their support. Consequently their refusal is elevated to a main theme. What we have always accepted now becomes despicable. At the end of the film, when Cooper takes off his badge and drops it into the dirt in the middle of the street, his action is not inexplicable or reprehensible. We do not disavow it. We too have begun to doubt the value of our inherited vision: is the community for which so much has been sacrificed worth the cost? Now that we have annihilated our foreign enemies, why isn't our natural goodness shining through? Could it be that the fault has been partially within ourselves?

The source of our present suffering, at least in part, is to be found somewhere within our own community. This is a working assumption of both the "detective" story, which has been with us for over a century, and the "gangster" movies, which first appeared in the early 1930's.[15] Gangster and detective stories alike reveal our frustrations and fears in a life more and more dominated by urbanization. In the urban environment, good townspeople and evil outlaws all live together. In the detective story someone has broken the pattern of law and order by committing a crime. If we are to continue to live together in relative peace, the perpetrator must be discovered and brought to justice. This process is thought to mend the tear in the social fabric. Whereas the detective-story villain may be a normally respectable member of the community, the gangster film criminal is a professional outlaw whose life is dedicated to pillaging the community for personal advantage.

The film *Bad Day at Black Rock* (1955) merges the Western form with the detective story. There had been detective films prior to 1955, but they had lacked the ritual dramatic power of the Western form. In *Bad Day*, the focal issue is a crime committed in the past, requiring that the hero, Spencer Tracy, play detective as well as deliverer. The villains can be anyone *in* the community. Here we have an element of the anti-Western: some of the people *within* the community are the villains. Unlike both the classic Western and its urban cousin the gangster film, the villains are not professional thieves or murderers whose crimes are for financial gain or social status. In *Bad Day at Black Rock* the villains are respectable, hardworking members of the community whose only crime is a single act of violence in the recent past.[16]

Bad Day is about a man named McCready (played by Spencer Tracy). Having lost an arm in the recently concluded Second World War, he comes to Black Rock to present a medal for bravery to the father of the Japanese-American boy who threw himself on a grenade to save Tracy's life. The boy was killed and Tracy lost only his arm. The community of Black Rock, situated in the barren plains east of the Rocky Mountains, resembles the typical frontier town of the classic Western. Something is eating at the collective conscience of this American town, something that makes them afraid of strangers. Tracy is greeted with hostility and lack of cooperation at every turn. Komoko, the Japanese-American farmer, is dead, apparently the victim of a sudden and unexplained fire which destroyed his homestead four years ago. Since the film's present is 1945, the "tragedy" occurred shortly after Pearl Harbor in 1941. As it turns out, Komoko was murdered by a mob of townspeople inflamed by a leading citizen (Robert Ryan) and his two cronies (Ernest Borgnine and Lee Marvin). The hotel manager (John Erickson) reluctantly participated and the cowardly sheriff (Dean Jagger) pretended not to notice. In the final showdown when Tracy must face Ryan, Erickson and Jagger redeem themselves by helping to capture Marvin and Borgnine.

While its villains are citizens of the community, *Bad Day at Black Rock* virtually smothers its anti-Western elements in reasserting the stability of the classic Western formula.[17] The Western eventually triumphs over the threat of the anti-Western. The villains may be in our midst, but we can weed them out and be whole again. The community of Black Rock is basically good, and will continue to be so after the few "bad apples" receive their due. As Tracy boards the train at the end of the film, he hands the medal intended for Komoko over to Walter Brennan, representing the town's "good" citizens. Absent most of the film, we now see them lined up in the background.

Brennan: "Can we have the medal?"
Tracy: "What will you do with it?" [*paraphrase*]
Brennan: "We'll build on it."

From Suspicions to Cynicism and Vengeance

From its early tentative statements in *High Noon* and *Bad Day at Black Rock*, the anti-Western film progressed (or regressed) in a logical direction. All three elements of the Western cast—townspeople, hero, villain—were affected. The immoral character of the townspeople reached such depths that an attempt at soul-purifying judgment became inevitable. The hero's fate inspired laments, and occasionally a vague criticism. The villain, hated in the Western, replaced the hero in the anti-Western. Let us look briefly at this turnabout world.

Evil in the Community. The townspeople, always good and innocent, suddenly appear not only evil and guilty, but irredeemably so. In John Ford's *Stagecoach* (1939) a motley group of social misfits prove in the end to be essentially good, caring human beings, dignifying deliverer John Wayne's defense of their lives. Director Martin Ritt tells the same story in *Hombre* (1967), except that the stagecoach passengers in Ritt's film wallow in criminal corruption and self-seeking cowardice. When hero-deliverer Paul Newman dies to save them, his death, far from ennobling, shocks and saddens us. This community is not redeemed—the deliverer's death is a tragic waste.

David Miller's *Lonely Are the Brave* (1962), a far more devastating anti-Western, shared little of *Hombre*'s popular success. Recently, however, its prophetic message has been "discovered," and the film raised from obscurity to cult film status. Apparently, what could not be faced in 1962 we now admit. *Lonely* is the story of a cowboy (Kirk Douglas) who suddenly discovers that

he is an individual in a world where the individual is no
longer respected. In the impersonal, dehumanized
world of contemporary civilization, Douglas is the "last
individual." The totalitarian reach of modern society is
almost complete. The source of evil is no longer external to the community, it is the community itself. This
society locks away in jail a classic inheritor-of-the-torch
figure, his only crime one of compassion: he gave first
aid to fleeing Mexican migrant workers being hunted
by the police. Douglas breaks into the jail to help his
buddy break out. There he encounters one of society's
keepers, a viciously sadistic prison guard.

Among the prisoners a grubby, unshaven clergyman
sits preaching about the sinful condition of the other
prisoners. Noticing that the preacher is himself dressed
in prison garb, a fellow inmate asks the clergyman how
he got into prison. The preacher confesses that although he had the "call," women were his downfall. So
much for the community's religious institutions.

The guardians of public safety and order fare no
better. When Douglas escapes, a sardonic police chief,
played by Walter Matthau, pursues him. Matthau is
surrounded by stupid and incompetent police-clerk
types whose good cheer and enthusiasm ironically be-
lie the unworkability of the institution they supposedly operate. Matthau, himself a disgustedly reluctant participant in the modern society, cheers from his
office window as the town mongrel works his way
down Main Street urinating on the bank and the post
office. Though seriously trying to catch the fleeing
"criminal," Matthau secretly cheers him on, and
smirks in satisfaction when Douglas temporarily escapes over the border. The military join the search to

give their reserves a little field practice.

A community of vicious prison guards, hypocritical moral leaders, stuffy and unworkable organizations, and insensitive war-game enthusiasts is lost already. Judgment seems much more appropriate than redemption.

High Plains Drifter provides the judgment. With stunning photography and highly stylized visual symbolism, it places the anti-Western critique of the townspeople in a new kind of eschatological setting. Eastwood appears not as the typical classic Western redeemer-hero, but as the apocalyptic Christ of the Last Judgment. The story line is simple. The town in question had a young, honest sheriff who turned out to be more honest than was desired. Certain townspeople whose mine operations are surreptitiously on government property hired three thugs to kill the sheriff. Late one night, as most of the town watched from the shadows, the three desperadoes whipped the young sheriff to death on Main Street. The three killers did not go away, however, much to the displeasure of the townspeople, who finally had them drugged and hauled off to prison. All this occurs before the film begins. We learn of it in brief flashbacks.

As the film opens, Eastwood rides into town, a bearded drifter, a resurrected version of the murdered young sheriff. He is sufficiently transformed that only a few of the better townspeople see in him something of the former sheriff. At one level, the story reminds us of *High Noon,* because the town hires Eastwood to protect them from the three desperadoes whose prison term is up and whose threats to return for vengeance terrify the townspeople. At another level, Eastwood engineers the destruction of the town he is hired to pro-

tect, while seeming to prepare it to face the return of
the killers. Under the terms of his contract Eastwood is
to have anything he wants. Subsequently, he gives blan-
kets to impoverished Indians and candy to their kids.
He treats the whole town to drinks in the local bar; he
buys several pairs of expensive boots at the local leather
shop. Since the hotel owner doesn't sell things, Eastwood sleeps with his wife (played sympathetically by
Verna Bloom). He takes away the sheriff's badge and
the mayor's hat and transfers the symbols of office as
well as their responsibilities to a midget, the butt of the
town's jokes.

Appropriately climaxing this mockery, Eastwood has
the town inhabitants literally paint the whole town red,
while he changes the name of the town to "Hell." Then,
he stations the men on rooftops with rifles while the rest
of the town stands by long picnic tables heaped with
hot, delicious food, under a sign saying "Welcome
Home, Boys." As the killers ride storming into town,
trampling the banquet facilities, Eastwood rides calmly
out the other side and away into the distance. Left to
their own cowardice and hypocrisy, the townspeople
fall apart. They are decimated by the outlaws, who set
fire to the town. Amid the flames of Hell itself, a shadowy Eastwood appears like a specter to kill the outlaws
one by one. The next day he rides out of town, past the
burned-out buildings, past the remaining members of
the town who stand staring in shocked disbelief. As he
rides out, he passes a tombstone on the grave of the
former sheriff. The epitaph under the sheriff's name
reads "Rest in Peace."

The Hero, Unappreciated and Unloved. Criticism of
the townspeople often cuts in two directions. Their un-

redeemable evil intentions reflect on the hero-deliverer's task and image. In *Hombre,* the hero's sacrificial act fails to satisfy its purpose. *Lonely Are the Brave*'s cowboy, having escaped the posse, dies mute and in disbelief on a rain-swept highway, having been run down by a trailer truck full of privies (driven, in prophetic irony, by Carroll O'Connor of Archie Bunker fame). The community's recalcitrant sinfulness reduces the hero's life and death to meaninglessness.

The Western requires that the hero-deliverer receive the active support of two good townspeople—the inheritor of the torch and the virtuous woman who is wife/mother/homemaker in the community. Altering the images of these people, the anti-Western successfully destroys the hero-deliverer's credibility. In *The Man Who Shot Liberty Valance* (1962), John Ford tells us that the really rugged individual hero whose sacrifices had built this country is a forgotten and unappreciated man. Meanwhile, the politicians, bumbling and inept at coping with real evil, yet superficially slick and attractive, usurp the credit for delivering the community. Ford cast John Wayne as Tom Doniphon, the hero, Lee Marvin as the villain Liberty Valance (simplistic symbolism, even for Ford), and Jimmy Stewart as Ransom Stoddard, inheritor of the torch. The plot hinges on the shooting of Marvin, supposedly by Stewart but actually by Wayne. Stewart is an Eastern lawyer, fumbling and stodgy, to whom, according to Ford, we have ransomed the best of our heritage. Marvin is the classic villain, mean, vicious, crude—as uncivilized as they come. Wayne (playing, of course, John Wayne) shoots Marvin from an alley, but it appears that Stewart, who is confronting Marvin on Main Street, has killed

the villain. Even Stewart thinks so. Wayne does nothing
to correct the mistaken impression. The fame and noto-
riety Stewart receives propel him into the governorship
of the state. Meanwhile, the hero-deliverer who actually killed the villain dies a pauper, unknown and forgotten.

In 1966, satirist-director Richard Brooks neatly mas-
queraded an attack on John Ford's classic 1959 Western
The Searchers within an action thriller called *The
Professionals.* In *The Searchers,* the film John Wayne
calls his favorite movie role, Wayne and his compatriots
rescue kidnapped white women from wild, perverse,
and savage Indians. In *The Professionals,* the screen's
most exciting team of professional gunfighters[18] Burt
Lancaster, Lee Marvin, Robert Ryan, and Woody
Strode—march into Mexico to rescue wealthy rancher
Ralph Bellamy's beautiful wife (Claudia Cardinale)
from her savage kidnapper, Mexican bandit Jack Palance. After much derring-do and risking of life and
limb, our heroes reach the girl only to discover that the
kidnapping was a farce! She is in love with Palance and
must be dragged kicking and screaming back to her
husband! The "heroes" come off as fools; the "good"
woman they are sent to rescue prefers the excitement
of the outlaw band to the decadent boredom of the rich
and corrupt community.

Reverence for the Outlaw. There is no use beating a
dead horse. If the townspeople are no good, and if we
can no longer believe in the traditional hero-deliverer,
to whom can we turn for excitement and adventure? Of
the three central characters of the Western drama, only
the villain is left. Can the villain be the hero? Once the
simplistic distinction been good and evil has been eradi-

cated, and we have begun to live with evil in the towns-people, the evil of the outlaw doesn't seem quite so extreme. Everything is relative. When life in the community becomes claustrophobic, deadening and depressing, the free, spontaneous life of the outlaw band may begin to look pretty attractive.

The most attractive feature of outlaw life has always been male comradeship. Americans still respect the boys-will-be-boys philosophy which continuously produces the adolescent male adult in American society. (Imagine, for instance, the roles of Trapper and Hawkeye in *M*A*S*H* played by women! Impossible!) The incredible success of "reverence for the outlaw" cannot be explained solely on anti-Western grounds. But the anti-Western provided a vehicle for shifting male comradeship to center stage. Of the outlaw anti-Westerns, we will examine three of the most popular: *Butch Cassidy and the Sundance Kid, The Wild Bunch,* and *The Sting.*

All three present criminals sympathetically, reveling in their freewheeling, fun-filled life *(Butch Cassidy)*, lamenting the demise of their fellowship *(The Wild Bunch)*, or leaning on the relativity of good and evil by heroically destroying even bigger crooks *(The Sting)*. In each film the hero-villains are shot down in the end, though some variation of a rationale or twist is added to ennoble the death scene itself. In *Butch Cassidy and the Sundance Kid,* Paul Newman and Robert Redford are finally trapped by the Mexican militia and killed. But they die in the incredible act of charging the overwhelming force gathered against them, defying death itself.[19] In *The Wild Bunch,* Pike Bishop (William Holden) and his gang are massacred by the soldiers of the Mexican bandit Mapache. We see most of them die, one by one—Holden, for example, is shot in the back by the young Mexican woman he slept with the night before. But they take scores with them, including Mapache himself. They die "doing what they must do," just like the Western hero. One of their gang, a young boy named Angel, has been arrested and beaten by Mapache. The gang know that their mission is suicidal but they demand Angel's release. When Mapache slits Angel's throat right in front of them the shooting begins. We lament not only the passing of the outlaw gang, but the end of the comradeship and free life they represented. And we respect the code by which they lived. Bishop says at one point: "We're gonna stick together, all of us. . . . When you side with a man you stay with him. If you can't do that you're worse than some animal." Their loyalty to each other defies even death; and they die defending that commitment.

In *The Sting,* Newman and Redford team up again in the same "older brother–younger brother" relationship they started in *Butch Cassidy.* They aim to fleece a millionaire syndicate man out of four hundred thousand dollars. The motive is the same as that of *The Wild Bunch:* one of their own, a black confidence artist, has been killed by the syndicate. In the ending Newman shoots Redford, but it turns out to be a ruse, fooling both the syndicate chief and the movie audience. Newman can't be allowed to shoot Redford—good grief! The confidence men who help pull off the hoax have Runyonesque hearts of gold. Compared to the evil syndicate head (Robert Shaw) and the bullyish cop who pursues Redford, these small-time confidence men are heroes. The classic Western's simplistic distinction between good and evil is maintained in *The Sting.* In real life such characters are some of the worst parasites living off the social order, swindling sixty-two-year-old widows out of their life savings. But in *The Sting* such are heroes.

The roles assigned to women in these films are those least threatening to male-male relationships. The women are typecast submissives, offering free and irre-sponsible sex, cardboard versions of *macho* favorites. In *Butch Cassidy* there is only one female role, Sundance's mistress, Etta Place, played by Katharine Ross. Ms. Place stays in her place, cooking, keeping house, and occasionally providing a third gun. She never com-plains. She romps on a bicycle with Butch, and she mocks an "outlaw rapes the schoolmarm" situation with Sundance, her lover. But she never comes between them or tries to domesticate Sundance. In *The Wild Bunch* there are few women. Two enormously fat and buxom Mexican whores romp with the scurviest of the Bunch in a huge wine vat. Angel, the only one of the gang with anything resembling a "sweetheart," shoots his woman for fooling around with Mapache, the bandit chief. Pike Bishop sleeps with a beautiful young Mexi-can woman provided by Mapache, but we see only the scene of his arising the next morning, guiltily putting some money on the table as he watches the hatred in her eyes. In *The Sting* Paul Newman's girl is the madam of a house of prostitution, who, when not sleeping with Newman, waits on the men as they play poker and make plans. The other woman in *The Sting* is a profes-sional killer, called simply Salinas. The audience hears only the name and is caught in a male chauvinist as-sumption that the killer is a male. We are surprised when this woman, whom we have seen waiting tables in a local eatery, turns out to be a killer. Such a turning of the tables on our own prejudices might have been a clever lesson and a valuable quality in the film, except that we soon remember she slept with Redford the night before. Even a professional killer, if female, is unable to resist the charms of supermale Redford.[20] Neither woman is a threat via romance and marriage to the Newman-Redford relationship. Salinas, a threat to Redford as his killer, is herself eliminated by a male killer hired by Newman to keep Redford safe.

One last comment on the outlaw as hero in the anti-Western. Often the outlaw gang, however heroic, is pursued by a posse of civilized society. They are bent on wiping out the last remnant of free-roaming, spontaneous males, whose loyalty is restricted to the fellowship they represent or to the code for which they live. Such outlaw-heroes are dangerous to the faceless anonymity of the New Heaven promised by modern civilization. Butch and Sundance are relentlessly pursued by a posse they are unable to lose. Butch is prompted to say at one point, "Who *are* those guys?"[21] In *Joe Kidd*, Clint Eastwood is hired by a posse to help them track a band of Mexican revolutionaries. As the film develops, Eastwood comes to ask Butch's question of the "posse" with which he rides. The "revolutionaries" turn out to be fighting for legal rights ruthlessly taken from them, and the posse is revealed to be a group of professional killers and bounty hunters sent to murder the chief of the rebels. In *The Wild Bunch*, Bishop's gang is hunted throughout by a scraggly group of mercenaries, whose avarice and infighting stand in striking contrast to the code of honor of the Bunch. In *The Sting*, Redford is hunted by the mob and by the faceless hired killer, Salinas, narrowly escaping time after time. Not only is the comradeship and freedom of the outlaw band attractive to the tied-down, domesticated male of modern society, but such attractiveness is dangerous and must be destroyed, once and for all.

THE COMPLEAT ANTI-WESTERN:
McCabe and Mrs. Miller

In the years between *M*A*S*H* and *Nashville,* director Robert Altman brought out a relatively unappreciated but landmark film, *McCabe and Mrs. Miller* (1971). Critically acclaimed and commercially successful, it is now barely remembered. This is most unfortunate, for *McCabe and Mrs. Miller* is the most incisive and thoroughgoing attack on the classic Western formula yet to appear.[22] Most anti-Western films treat only the *dominant* cultural belief system, focusing on the present and future goodness of the *community* and its final fulfillment. *McCabe and Mrs. Miller* takes on the *subdominant* belief system as well—the image of *individual* humanity represented by the hero. *McCabe and Mrs. Miller* is about the beginning, growth, and final establishment of a community. It is also the story of the rise and fall of "deliverer" John McCabe, verging on the complete demythologizing of the hero.

There are several thinly veiled, overtly religious references in this film.[23] John McCabe and Mrs. Miller is obviously not far from Jesus Christ and Mary Magdalene. McCabe arrives on the scene to Leonard Cohen's sound-track line, "Joseph looking for a manger." He immediately establishes rapport with the shabby min-

ers with his glib talk and cool presence. He passes
around a flask to solidify their communion. Rumor has
it that he is fast with a gun, which he isn't. He neither
affirms nor denies what the crowd says about him. But
it is clear that they wish him to be someone else. Mary
Magdalene is a prostitute; Mrs. Miller is a high-class
madam. Eventually McCabe dies fighting for the town,
a battle he does not want to fight. Even though he dies
victoriously, having killed the mining company thugs,
his death is futile and meaningless. The community is
off tending to other affairs, and control of the town by
the mining company is inevitable anyway. One could
do a lot with the Christological assumptions and assertions in this film.

Apropos of the anti-Western, *McCabe and Mrs.
Miller* follows, at least in outline, the classic Western
form. It is the story of the transformation of a dank,
dark, and dismal mining community of makeshift tents
and shacks whose only significant communal gathering
place is Sheehan's bar. It becomes a town of future
prosperity, respectability, and concern for more traditionally proper places of established community behavior, in this case the local Presbyterian church whose
name the original settlement ironically bears. When
McCabe (Warren Beatty) first rides into the town of
Presbyterian Church, the scaffolding of the half-com-
pleted building looms in the background. In the final
scene, while McCabe lies dying in the snow the townspeople gather together to try to save the now burning
church from destruction.[24] The people of the new community come of age when they shift their attention
from Sheehan's bar to the Presbyterian church. Thus,
superficially at least, the outline of the film mirrors the

pattern of the classic Western: a community whose survival is at stake, a heroic figure who shoots it out with evil interlopers, and the realization of the peaceful, prosperous future dream of the human community.

The mark of the anti-Western intervenes as this drama unfolds. Although we get what we thought we wanted, somehow we feel rotten rather than redeemed. McCabe gets the people of Presbyterian Church moving by appealing to and playing upon their worst instincts. He wins their confidence and admiration with dirty jokes. The first real community business empire, which McCabe established, is a whorehouse. The completion of the outside of the church, and the securing of the cross to the steeple, coincide with the arrival of McCabe's first prostitutes. Nothing more is ever done on the church. When McCabe enters it in the final scenes, as he searches for a place of advantage against the killers, we see that the inside of the church is a mass of decayed and rusting building materials, with the pathetic minister living like a churchmouse amid the debris. The prostitution business, however, moves into lush quarters erected by the men of the town. Mrs. Miller's arrival brings order, bookkeeping, health regulations, and truly beautiful prostitutes to inhabit the newly furbished building. Mrs. Miller has added the requisite structure to McCabe's spunk and initiative. The mining camp has taken a definitive step toward community. The new "sportin' house" is a place of civilized and mannered social graces—you have to take a bath before you are admitted.

Director Altman's keen understanding of the Western–anti-Western debate, and his grasp of the essential elements of each, make the central scene of the film forceful and incisive. The community, originally the sloppy, gross fellowship of Sheehan's bar, is marked in its fulfilled stage by the resourceful effort to fight the fire in the church. At the halfway point, however, the community is gathered for a birthday party in the gay and festive atmosphere of the new brothel. Gone forever is the coarse conversation, the unkempt dress and behavior, of the old community; a more civilized, mannered society has begun to take its place. But Altman's irony is not lost. The birthday celebration is held at Christmastime—the music at the party makes this evident. However, the celebration is not for the birth of the Christ-child, but for one of the Seattle whores. The festivities take place not in the church, which stands externally completed and internally a shambles, but in the richly decorated bordello.

Between the brothel party and the climax of the film, one event stands out as symbolic of the moral and spiritual decline of the town. A mining company has become interested in locating here and has sent business representatives and company thugs to visit the community. Coincidental to their visit, Altman introduces a young cowboy who is drifting through the town and visits the whorehouse. No one could be more representative of the pure innocence of the West than this lad. His Christlike looks and naïve manner immediately attract everyone. But when one of the company hoodlums kills the drifter for no reason at all, no one in the community raises a word of protest. Gary Engle describes the situation eloquently:

The cowboy, . . . the one character in the film most reminiscent of a conventional Western type, is senselessly killed. . . . This unprovoked murder is the convincing proof of the evil of the mining company and its envoys. The shots of the cowboy's body floating face up in the pond are intercut with shots of the townspeople standing on the balcony of the hotel, their hands in their pockets, having refused to intervene in the killing or respond to the brutality. . . . The unprecedented violence of this scene, emphasized by the use of slow motion, demands judgment on the part of the audience; and the judgment which Altman wishes us to make seems absolutely clear. By failing to respond the town has identified itself with the killers and has exposed the acceptance of savagery which belies the idea of social progress. This suggests that the notion of progress is hypocritical. It is the merciless, professional brutality of the envoys to which the townspeople sheepishly submit. They reveal by this submission that the town has not progressed away from evil, but has grown toward it. At its worst social progress is a moral decline. At its best it is merely a series of external changes which fail to alter man's basic nature.[25]

Interpretations of the state of the community of Presbyterian Church at the end of the film are legion.[26] But they all have at least this observation in common: Altman's view of the passing of the community from a fledgling people to a full-fledged and realized community is laced with irony, and is anti-Western to the core. They fight to save the Presbyterian church which they have hitherto virtually ignored. So their odyssey to full community status is marked by the progression from bar to brothel to church. Not bad. But they work to preserve a social institution which is nothing more than a shell. The minister is already dead, his body inside the burning building. Meanwhile, the man who made all of this possible, and who has just shot it out with three desperadoes, lies in the snow wounded and dying, unaided. His sacrifice is unwitnessed, unappreciated, ignored. With such a triumph of human insensitivity, the community enters into its reward. As Ralph Brauer puts it, the town is shown putting out the fire in the church while McCabe struggles to put out the fire in Presbyterian Church. And loses.[27]

Some mention of *McCabe and Mrs. Miller*'s critique of the role of women in the classic Western should be noted to supplement what we have previously said.[28] Altman has not only confounded the traditional distinction between the good- and the bad-girl townsperson, but he has attacked both images. Mrs. Miller (Julie Christie), the female star of the film, combines the sexual promiscuity of the bad girl with the guts, brains, and ingenuity of the good girl. She is, in effect, the person who finally and firmly establishes ordered business prosperity in Presbyterian Church. Like Quaker Grace Kelly in *High Noon,* she tries to keep the hero from a worthless shoot-out with three killers. Unlike good-girl Kelly, she does not finally come to the hero's assistance, but hides in the temporary forgetfulness of an opium den while McCabe bleeds to death in the snow outside her door. In a symbolic moment—a tribute to Altman's genius—Mrs. Miller subverts one of civilized society's most cherished and sacred institutions, the family. In the classic Western the good girl is the bedrock of the future of civilization because she is wife and mother. In *McCabe and Mrs. Miller,* the first good-girl wife-type to arrive in Presbyterian Church is a mail-order bride. When the woman's husband is killed in a street brawl, Mrs. Miller doesn't even wait until the funeral services are over before she begins to recruit the woman for her brothel. To the great satisfaction of the secret desires of all the audience's males, she succeeds.

McCabe and Mrs. Miller is as much the unmasking of the Western hero as it is the uncovering of the dirty underside of modern civilization. In his characterization of McCabe, Altman follows the pattern he used in dealing with the progress of the community. He sets the anti-Western elements like counterpoint against a classic Western melody. To open the film, McCabe rides into town, a mysterious stranger with a mysterious and rumored past, in much the same way the more traditional hero does. At the conclusion McCabe shoots it out with three hired killers who have come to town to kill him, as Gary Cooper does in *High Noon.* He is even victorious over his enemies, though, like Shane, he is mortally wounded.[29]

Here, however, the Western formula ends. McCabe engages in racial slurs while discussing the Chinese workers with Sheehan.[30] He imports three filthy, pathetic whores to start his business adventures. Only the traditional villain would be caught in the company of such creatures, much less pimping for them. McCabe, whose humor seems winning and enjoyable in Sheehan's bar and in the company of the miners, is awkward and sophomoric in his meeting with the educated representatives of the mining company. The jokes are the same in both instances: what we first interpreted as spontaneous wit is revealed as little more than the vest-pocket reservoir of a frequent after-dinner speaker. Though McCabe seems to have taken control of the town and established himself as one of its leaders, he cannot match the sophistication and intelligence of

Mrs. Miller. He is flabbergasted by the rapid-fire fashion in which she bombards him with what he doesn't know about the brothel business. It is her *savoir-faire* which really makes their business endeavor a success. Her control of their future is evident when he starts following her orders (though he hides this from the town) and when he falls madly in love with her. Though the image of the traditional Western hero is one of sophistication, of knowing what to do and how to act in every situation, McCabe dangerously misjudges the mining company officials and, though he really wants to sell out, quotes them a ridiculously high price. He is then unwilling to admit that the thugs who come to kill him are anything but new negotiators for his property. In a scene that parodies and reverses the relationship of Eastern lawyer Ransom Stoddard (Jimmy Stewart) and Western hero Tom Doniphon (John Wayne) in *The Man Who Shot Liberty Valance,* McCabe is reduced to stammering bewilderment by an Eastern lawyer's overblown and pretentious patriotic rhetoric.

The final scenes underscore all the doubts and fears raised in our minds about this "hero." McCabe shoots it out with the three mining thugs and kills them all. But the attention of the community, the symbolic act by which their dreams are realized, is elsewhere—in saving the burning church. McCabe's fight stands cut off from the meaning of the future of the community, a community more concerned with buildings than with human beings. Gary Engle argues convincingly for the anti-Western character of McCabe's death:

First, nothing is gained by McCabe's elimination of the killers. The mining company remains. It is worth stressing that McCabe's own death leaves the company free to plunder the resources of the town. Secondly, McCabe does not fight on behalf of the community. Nor does he fight out of devotion to any ideal set of values. His only motive for accepting involvement with the company is financial gain; and his only motive for eventually fighting them is self-preservation. Finally his actions cannot be considered heroic in the sense that he might represent the individual who achieves nobility by engaging in a futile attempt to wrestle with fate; for we are made to see that his death is unnecessary. . . . His character has not been exalted, but rather exposed and discredited throughout the course of the story. At the moment of his death he is not acting at the peak of heroism, but rather at the nadir of anti-heroism.[31]

McCabe is overwhelmed, and though he is far from heroic in character, his last thoughts are probably analogous to those of Butch Cassidy: "Who *are* those guys?"

THE RETURN OF THE DOMINANT-BELIEF-SYSTEM WESTERN

The golden age of the anti-Western seems to be drawing to a close. We will never again be without it; we cannot go back to the naïveté of our former innocence. But the last few years have witnessed the phenomenal popularity of four films whose structure is clearly the classic Western. The dominant American belief system has not gone away. With its simplistic distinctions between good and evil, its confidence that evil is external and those plagued by it are pure, its communal vision of salvation, its trust in the direct and violent act of the individual-deliverer as redemptive—the dominant

American belief system and its ritual form, the Western, is with us again.

The four films are: *Walking Tall,*[32] the story of Tennessee Sheriff Buford Pusser's fight to cleanse McNairy County, Tennessee; *Billy Jack* and *The Trial of Billy Jack,* parts two and three of the Laughlin family tale of an ex-Green Beret/kung-fu champion and his heroic battle against business and government corruption; and *Death Wish,* the story of the awakening of a New York vigilante who in his real life identity is a mild-mannered architect. We have called the Billy Jack stories a trilogy in order to include *Born Losers,* a mid-sixties motorcycle movie, the film in which the character "Billy Jack" first appeared.

Walking Tall and *Billy Jack* were grass-roots blockbusters that rose like phoenixes in the small-town Midwest from the ashes of disastrous Eastern city first runs. *Death Wish* rode to financial success partially on the now superstar appeal of its leading man, Charles Bronson. *The Trial of Billy Jack* piggybacked on the success of *Billy Jack,* continuing the story begun there. In 1973, *Walking Tall* was eighteenth on the list of top-grossing motion pictures, one slot ahead of the *reissue* of *Billy Jack. Born Losers* has been a top-draw favorite at drive-ins for several years, and was released into a successful theater run in 1974. There is little argument that someone is buying whatever these films are selling.

The startling aspect of the success of these films is their unabashed return to the themes of the classic American Western form. All three films (we will consider the Billy Jack trilogy as one film, since thematically all three films are of a piece) present a break in the peace and harmony of the community by some force

external to those who are suffering. In *Walking Tall,*
Buford returns to a small Tennessee town beset by a
syndicate gambling and vice operation which threatens
to undermine the community's future. The syndicate
has set up its own "community" on the edge of town:
in contrast to the good women of the town whose lives
are spent maintaining traditional American homes, the
women of the syndicate "community" are prostitutes,
women of dubious moral value, who ply their trade in
mobile homes adjoining the gambling casino. The
townspeople remain essentially innocent, and clearly
good, in contrast to the vicious crime-syndicate villains.
Death Wish identifies the good townspeople as Middle
American city dwellers. The villains become muggers
and rapists, vermin who inhabit the city but are not
really considered responsible citizens, much less human
beings. The sexual anxiety of the classic Western form
—"those perverse and filthy outlaws are after our clean
and pious women"—is raised in *Death Wish* from the
traditionally implicit level to harsh and explicit visual
detail. The wife of the architect hero is murdered by
muggers who simultaneously sexually assault his
twenty-five-year-old daughter. Though this is the only
sexual act by muggers in the entire film, its impact
marks the film throughout.

The Billy Jack trilogy involves a shift from the first
film, *Born Loser,* to *Billy Jack* and *The Trial of Billy
Jack.* In *Born Losers,* a motorcycle gang, clearly both
evil and external to the town community, terrorizes an
essentially good townspeople—and especially their
teen-age daughters. *Billy Jack* and its sequel use the
urbanized setting: good guys and bad guys all live in the
same "community." Still, these films simplistically dis-

tinguish between two communities—the United States
and the freedom school. The larger community, the
United States, is clearly the source of evil. Its business,
political, and military leaders are the villains. The freedom school community of loving, beautiful, always well-
intentioned flower children struggles to survive while
exposing the "other" community as hypocritical and
decadent. Town rednecks menace them in the first film;
the FBI and National Guard assault them in the second.
All three films plainly preach the classic Western form:
those who have the problem are not themselves its
source.

As in the classic Western, these recent films spotlight
the hero as deliverer, the one whose actions save the
community by annihilating or neutralizing the community's foe. In the anti-Western more attention was
devoted to the subdominant cultural belief system
represented in the personal image of the hero as the
self-contained ("sophisticated") individual. In *Walking
Tall*, Buford's bloody battering of the syndicate forces
aims at preserving a decent, law-abiding community.
The jury in his subsequent trial takes five minutes to
find him not guilty, given the choice between the evidence for the prosecution (a group of broken-boned,
cast-enclosed, and bandage-wrapped casino operators)
and Buford's plea of "self-defense." Arguing his own
case, he rips off his shirt to expose the multiple scars of
wounds inflicted by the syndicate men. He says that the
only protection the jury citizens have from the same
treatment is affirmation of his own act of retaliation.
The townspeople reinforce the jury's decision by elect-
ing Buford sheriff. In *Death Wish*, the architect-
vigilante becomes a national hero, meriting not only

banner headlines in the New York City press, but cover
stories in *Newsweek* and *Time.* The New York City police finally discover the vigilante's identity, but rather
than arrest him they tell him to get his firm to transfer
him to another city! Billy Jack appears mysteriously
from the mist to aid the freedom school children in
Billy Jack, the heroine in *Born Losers,* and the Indians
in *The Trial of Billy Jack.* Billy Jack even gives himself
up to the authorities in *Billy Jack* in exchange for government protection and support of the freedom school.
In both *Billy Jack* and the subsequent *Trial* film, one of
the folk-singing members of freedom school sings, "Are
you dying just for me, Billy Jack?"

In *Walking Tall* and the Billy Jack films, a towns-
woman reiterates the classic Western role for women.
Buford's wife (played by Elizabeth Hartman) argues
repeatedly against Buford's wearing (and presumably
using) a gun. Jean Roberts (played by Laughlin's real-
life wife, Delores Taylor), head of the freedom school
and Billy Jack's romantic interest, preaches pacifism (as
did Grace Kelly in *High Noon*). Hartman is the good,
faithful, stay-at-home wife, center of a family of small
children and grandparents; Taylor is an emancipated
schoolmarm. Sexual anxiety and fear for the future of
the community connect these films with what we said
above about *Death Wish.* In *Billy Jack,* Taylor is raped;
in *The Trial of Billy Jack,* national guardsmen shoot her
down and she ends the film paralyzed in a wheelchair.
In *Born Losers,* the heroine is raped and beaten. Syndicate villains murder Buford's wife in *Walking Tall.*

Death Wish has no heroine, since the hero's wife is
murdered early in the film, but it consciously employs
the Western form in other ways. The architect is unable

to accept the tragic end of his family. The police tell him it will be practically impossible to find the muggers who were responsible. Then he takes a business trip to the Southwest. His Western host is a man who respects space and natural beauty and who won't compromise the integrity of the land to cut costs on the housing project he is building. Upon hearing the architect's story, the Western builder contrasts the safety of the West with the city of muggers and rapists, and emphatically tells the architect how they would handle such criminals in the West. The architect returns to New York City to discover in his luggage a present from his Western host—a silver six-shooter. The vigilante is born. Toward the end of the film, when the police detective tells the wounded architect, "I want you out of town," the architect smiles and asks, "By sundown?"

Have we seen the end of the trend toward anti-Western criticism of the classic Western form? Are Americans beginning to renew their faith in the dominant belief system? Has the traditional Western form returned? Or are these films merely a release of the tension, frustration, and despair of the fiery and disruptive sixties? We can only wait and see, though the two hundredth anniversary celebration of the American Revolution may act as a catalyst for a return to the classic form.

4

Country Music:
THE SONGS
OF POPULAR CULTURE

Country music, or "country and western music," is the only uniquely adult successfully popular music in the United States.[33] Certainly it is the fastest-growing kind of music in American culture. Country performers who haven't been north of Nashville for decades are suddenly giving concerts in New York City's Carnegie Hall. Radio stations coast to coast are switching to an all-country format. Country-music bars proliferate in Northern cities; huge outdoor park concert facilities spring up, luring fans to all-day Sunday shows featuring the latest Nashville sensation. *Time* and *Newsweek* do cover stories on the resurgence. The Capital Music Hall in Wheeling, West Virginia (calling itself "Nashville North"), is swamped with enough ticket requests to fill their three-thousand-seat auditorium three times in one night for Merle Haggard, and five times in two consecutive nights for Johnny Cash. Records by distinctively country recording stars begin to be heard on all-music format radio stations; the stars themselves list over twenty-five of their number as millionaires. All this is testimony to the growing popularity of a type of music already reflecting value preferences of Americans. Let's look at those values.

THE FAMILY IN COUNTRY MUSIC

One of the most widely recorded country songs of all time is A. P. Carter's "Will the Circle Be Unbroken?" The song tells the story of a family whose center has become suddenly a meaningless void: the mother has died. She was not only the center around which the family gathered and had its good and bad times, she was also the source of the unity and strength that the family means to its members. Her death means not only loss of a loved one, or the final breaking of the umbilical cord of mother-child relations, but also that the family will begin to drift apart, flotsam upon a turbulent sea. Small wonder that such an event raised an aching question into the context of a simple faith.

The singer recalls the "cold and cloudy day" when she (he) was standing by the window and the chill of the day became a chill in the heart as she saw "the hearse come rollin' for to carry my mother away." By the graveside the despair of the loss of the mother breaks forth in tears "as they laid her in the grave." Back home the loss is magnified by the weeping and moaning of brothers and sisters. But the overwhelming tragedy of the song is constantly broken between the verses by the chorus, in which the question "Will the [family] circle be unbroken?" meets the affirmation of faith, that the best of all homes is the one found with God in eternal life.

Such sentiments may sound simple in a folksy way, or even corny to many. But they are of the essence of the belief-system values most dominant in country music. Superstar duet Porter Wagoner and Dolly Parton sang about the value of married life in the ballad "Together

Always." What begins in this world is projected into eternity, "beyond this world where you and I will be together always." Our worldly vow is not merely a togetherness here and now, but in heaven as well. What a contrast to the growing sentiment that wedding vows are temporary even *within* this life!

The Family and Its Source of Grace

The basic social unit in country music is the family. It is the source of stability, peace, rest, happiness—it is the basic source of salvation, of meaning, purpose, and fulfillment. At its center, the source of grace itself, is wife and mother. Country singers place her next to God —she is called an "angel." One sings, "Heaven is my woman's love," and tells us how he couldn't make it through the day if she didn't bracket the drudgery of daily work with morning and evening love. Charley Pride sings, "She's too good to be true, but she is." Jim Ed Brown tells us of a love that is so fulfilling it's "unbelievable love." The weary, discouraged, beaten-down male is told by Dolly Parton to "touch your woman, everything's going to be all right." Charlie Rich (called "the Silver Fox" for his full head of prematurely white hair) skyrocketed to fame when he won the Record of the Year award for clearly distinguishing the secular from the sacred space. Vividly the secular space of social affairs like "parties" is described as a place where some couples display their affections by hanging all over each other in public. Rich denounces those who might interpret his own relative inattentiveness to his "baby" at these affairs as a lack of pride. He contrasts such carrying on in public with his own devotion to his "baby" in the sacred space, behind the "closed doors" of the personal, private marriage relationship where "no one knows what goes on." In the sacred space it is nobody's business!

Tribute to the sanctity of the marriage contract and its significance for country music fans was the hit "We're Gonna Hold On." Tammy Wynette, the "Queen of Country Music," left her job as a hairdresser in Itawamba, Mississippi, and came to Nashville, not only to make it to the top of her profession, but to marry one of country music's longtime superstars, George Jones. It was the perfect marriage—"nobody" country girl marries star singer. Then rumors were heard that their marriage was in trouble. It couldn't be true, country fans sighed. Somehow Tammy and George got it back together, and to reassure the fans that the family of all families still existed released a duet assuring their fans of what the title of the song proclaimed: "We're Gonna Hold On." Scarcely a year later they were divorced.

Threats to the Family Circle

A great percentage of the music popular in the country field can be understood only within the perspective just presented. When the family and its source of grace, the wife-angel, are set in a belief-systems context, many other songs clearly identify sources of evil. If salvation is the family, evil is anything that threatens the peace, unity, or tranquillity of family life. We will look at five kinds of threats.

Alcohol

First, though not necessarily in intensity, is alcohol. Loretta Lynn, the "coal miner's daughter" who was a grandmother at twenty-nine, rivals Tammy Wynette for top female vocalist in country music. Several years ago she performed a little ditty, the words of which describe a situation familiar to every married adult. Her husband comes home late after a night out with the boys. He is drunk and ready for a little loving. But "liquor and love they just don't mix"; you can't have both the bottle and the warmth and tenderness of family love. Loretta says it all in a one-line warning: "Don't come home adrinkin' with loving on your mind." The bottle has been the downfall of many a good man. Jerry Lee Lewis sang of a man trapped by the bottle who finally realizes that his "baby" is gone. Though she had begged him to stay home, time after time he had disregarded her admonitions. The "closed doors" of the marriage are not compatible with the "swinging doors" of the barroom. Too late he finally admits that "what made Milwaukee famous has made a fool out of me."

The Honky-tonk

Those "swinging doors" introduce the second threat to the peace and unity of the family, one intimately connected with alcohol—the honky-tonk. When we can't blame the evil brew itself, we can point to the den of sin and corruption in which it is served. Littered with lost and wicked women, painted and powdered, where every time you try to leave someone plays another song or buys another round, the honky-tonk traps good men and perverts innocent women. It takes away your freedom—whole lives go down the drain with every beer.

Yet its gaudy sights and lowered lights hold the promise
of secret pleasures and strange thrills—obviously the
lair of the devil himself. There is some debate as to
which sex is more in league with the honky-tonk's for-
bidden, self-defeating pleasures, and thus more responsible for the lives lost therein. There is little argument,
however, with the known "fact" that the honky-tonk is
a major threat to the family as the chief cause of the
downfall of previously angelic wives. In "Close All the
Honky-tonks" the singer laments, not the fact that his
wife has deserted him, but rather that she is a captive
of the bright night life of the honky-tonk. His solution
is not a reformed life for her—she is essentially good.
Rather, if you "close all the honky-tonks," she will come
home on her own. The theory that the honky-tonk and
its attractions are the sole seducer of innocent angels
has been furiously debated in song many times over,
but no more classic protest exists than Kitty Wells's old
standard, "The Wild Side of Life." The strength of the
denials is usually a response to a distinctly male tendency to "look down" on these "fallen women," a tendency readily embraced by the threatened housewife
who fears the seductive allure of these honky-tonk angels. In "It Wasn't God Who Made Honky-tonk Angels,"
Kitty Wells points the finger elsewhere. Almost every
heart that's ever been broken was because "there always was a man to blame." And which men? Married
men, who "think they are still single," who have not
accepted the responsibility of the sanctity of the family
life. As she listens to the song on the jukebox, she
remembers not when she was a "trusted" wife, but
when she was a "trusting" wife. She did not desert the
marriage, she was seduced away from it in her trusting

innocence. She is essentially a "good girl" who was led astray by some deceiving man. This is not unusual. The fallen woman or honky-tonk angel is rarely considered responsible for her plight.

There are, I think, two reasons for this. We have here ritual, rather than personal biographies. Country music partakes in the basic American belief system by portraying the source of evil as external to the person or persons afflicted. Moreover, the sacred place of women in the family represented here cannot allow even an inherited sinfulness to reside in that treasured source of grace and happiness. Women are essentially good, and stray from the family only through innocent trust falsely placed and maliciously betrayed. Where there is truth and beauty and grace, there is also an unworldliness easily taken advantage of. This is one reason that "women's liberation" as a movement is basically alien to the view of life represented in country music. "Liberation" entails taking on worldliness, at once challenging the domain of the men and rejecting the angelic protective innocence that formerly was shelter and refuge for the man whose "worldliness" had become a weary burden. I suspect that the anxiety produced among many men by "women's liberation" was much more a fear of losing the latter source of grace than of having to fight off women in the marketplace. At least this is true for the Americans whose values are expressed in the popularity of country music.

The issue of whose palace of seduction the honky-tonk is has hardly been settled. A song written by Shel Silverstein calls the honky-tonk angel the "Queen of the Silver Dollar," and describes her as a seductress from outside the community. This wicked woman isn't from the neighborhood, but arrives on a "crosstown bus" from mysterious, unknown places. The men in the bar are represented as fools and jesters, flocking around her, drooling and squabbling with one another for her "favors." Again, the externality of evil: the woman as seductress, before whom no man can keep his wits or his wisdom, and in whose presence family is forgotten.

Is the honky-tonk such a den of pervasive iniquity that none can pass through its swinging doors without forsaking family, God, and country forever? Hardly, or honky-tonks could not survive as they do, and do quite heartily. The more responsible family man can handle them. Charlie Rich sang of the man who stops off after work for a couple of drinks "to let the five o'clock rush go by." He isn't there long before some lady at the bar starts "coming on" to him. But he knows this routine, and values his home situation more. So he "packs it on up, turns it around, and takes it on home."

Bad Companions

The third external force detrimental to the ongoing family is the influence of "bad companions." We've all known a few in our day—and our parents always pointed to a few of our favorite friends as such. Possibly the classic country song in this area is "I Washed My Hands in Muddy Water," popularized by Stonewall Jackson. After informing us that his father lectured him from the Macon, Georgia, jail to the effect that if "you keep your hands clean," you'll never "hear those blood-hounds on your trail," Jackson confesses he "fell in with bad companions," robbed a bank, was caught, and now is doing hard time.

More likely to threaten the family directly are those

"bad companions" who subvert the center of the family herself. In "Pick Me Up on Your Way Down," we hear of just such a situation. A man laments the loss of his wife to newfound, rich friends who have wined and dined her away from her family. But he clearly assigns the blame—"they" have changed her attitude, have made her different. For this, "they" can "take the blame" because, deep down inside, she is "still the same," basically good. She is still an angel, though fallen, through the influence of "bad companions."

Adultery

By far the most feared threat to family security is "slippin' around," more commonly known as adultery. More country records deal with this problem than with any other. "Loving on Back Streets, Living on Main," is such a common situation in country music that one hit portrayed a deceived husband as referring to songs he had heard all his life with a new attitude: "I Just Started Hating Cheating Songs Today." So close to the source of salvation do these songs come that they often touch chords deep in the mythical subconsciousness of the fans. Exemplary of such was a big record for Barbara Mandrell called "The Midnight Oil." This song describes a wife who is cheating on her husband with her boss (a warning to all husbands whose wives would like to go to work), and who is watching her husband's reactions in the mirror while she dresses. She imagines how dirty her guilt will make her feel when she returns home with "the midnight oil all over me." The midnight oil spreads its meaning to include a reference to sexual lubricants and to the most primeval source of religious dread, the stain that cannot be removed.[34]

When the sin is so central, even the justifications are interesting. So, occasionally, even adultery is committed for the best of reasons. Loretta Lynn made popular a song whose first line was spoken: "I'd like to introduce myself." Then the singer introduces herself as "the other woman in your husband's life." The rationalization that follows is especially interesting, because rather than counter the belief-system values we have been discussing, it reaffirms them as a defense. The whole town thinks that you, his wife, are the injured party, true blue and innocent, and that we, your husband and I, are a threat to the social sanctity of the family and its responsibilities. But note what the "other woman" says: "You know who was first to cheat on who." The wife is accused of being the first to break the family circle, giving her husband the "right" to seek someone who would be the source of grace and meaning to his life. I didn't steal his love from you, the other woman says—you never wanted it, so he gave it to me. We all know that the family in which we now live falls short of the idealized family, in the same way that the local congregation always falls short of what the church could and should be. There is an undeniable measure of convincing truth in this justification, even though the adultery defended is normally a threat to the family as source of salvation, and thus an evil by definition. As another song puts it: "Love is where you find it, when you find no love at home; And nothing's cold as ashes, after the fire is gone."

Adultery is a threat most felt by the wife, in country music. Songs that suggest a way of dealing with adultery are not rare, though hardly ever does one counsel to "throw the bum out," and along with the "bum," the marriage. Most offer one of two approaches to the problem: either go to the source of the problem, the other woman; or forget it, he'll get over it. Both of these are "save the marriage" solutions, though from different perspectives. Dealing directly with the other woman may involve extremes, from Dolly Parton's pleading with "Jolene" not to take her man, to Loretta Lynn's famous fight song, "You Ain't Woman Enough to Take My Man." She sings: "Women like you are a dime a dozen, You can buy them anywhere." Those are "fighting words," spurned by the "be patient, he'll come back to you" school whose champion is Tammy Wynette. She soared to stardom with "Stand by Your Man," one of the first of a string of country songs to be played on all-music radio stations. Your man may do a lot of things you don't understand (like keeping late hours, going on mysterious business trips), but stand by him, it'll be worth it in the long run. In addition to waiting, you might try getting him into bed, because "a lot of good loving will make everything all right." Joining with husband George, Tammy sang that though they had some problems, "we loved them away." (Apparently some weren't that easily resolved.) Even Loretta Lynn can occasionally be found responding to "Trouble in Paradise" with the same advice: "I'm gonna love him till the Devil goes away." Body contact beats holy water and incantations any day!

A male adulterer may be a threat, but then boys will be boys. A wandering wife is another story. Again the sacred place of woman as wife should be remembered. The "double standard" employed here has roots far deeper than socially conditioned male chauvinism. When the source of divine, saving grace goes sour, the result is more than destructive—it is demonic. Still, only those whose sense of vigilante justice endears to them *Walking Tall, Death Wish,* or Mickey Spillane can listen without a creeping chill in the spine to Porter Wagoner's hit "The Cold, Hard Facts of Life." In story form, Wagoner sings about a man who comes back early from a business trip and stops in the corner liquor store for some wine. While in the liquor store he overhears the man in front of him buying booze for a great party down the street. " 'Her husband's out of town and there's a party'; He winked as if to say, 'You know the rest.' " Following him down the street, the husband sees the man turn into the husband's own driveway. As he drives around the block in shock, the husband muses dejectedly that he is being taught the "cold, hard facts of life." Only because we are witnessing a desecration of the sacred place is the last verse acceptable to country-music fans. Bolstered by the alcoholic courage of the now-empty wine bottle, the husband enters the house, knife in hand, and slays the home-defiling wife. We are spared the details. We hear only the husband's jail-cell declaration of justice satisfied: "Who taught who the cold, hard facts of life?"

Evil Women

The fifth and final threat to the basic social unit is evil women. Women are essentially good in country music, as we have said. But there is a significant exception. There still flourishes in this country the fear of demonic, death-dealing women, descending from Eve, capable of ensnaring and enslaving the most noble of men. These women have a sexual power that no man's good intentions can resist. The women who use this power are considered evil, through and through. They are not fallen angels, they are incarnations of pure, seductive evil. Imagine the anxiety with which the everyday housewife hears Tammy Wynette's description in "Woman to Woman" of the enemy: she is beautiful, sexy, all woman, and "she can do things to a man you never dreamed a woman can do." Before such a woman, as Dolly Parton sings in "Jolene," one can only cower and beg, asking her not to take "the only man I'll ever love" when she can have her pick of the crop. The captive male is reduced to a vicious internal conflict, in which the "spirit is willing but the flesh is weak." The moral sense of the victim is often intact, as is his "will." But the body's addiction to the sexual drug supplied at the whim of the evil woman cripples both moral and spiritual powers, and interferes with all rational good judgment. A man in the grips of such a woman is trapped beyond his own self-control in "Easy Lovin'." "Easy Lovin' " is the tempting love of the easy woman, the loving without responsibility, without the burdens of family life. But the promise is the age-old one offered by the devil himself—easy wealth, success, love—for the final disposition of your soul.

Alcohol, honky-tonks, bad companions, adultery, and evil women—obstacles on the Way to salvation. Will the circle be unbroken? Country music tells us it will be broken, if we fail to counter and defeat these threats.

EDEN VS. SODOM AND GOMORRAH

Country music people have always had a well-founded distrust of the city and its ways. The city is crowded, polluted, noisy, dangerous. It is full of unnatu-

ral odors and artificial things, and worst of all, wall-to-
wall honky-tonks. The city has a way of gobbling good
people up and spitting them out rude and haughty, or
disgraced and humiliated. By contrast, the country is
green, natural, sweet-smelling, quiet, and full of good,
hard-working, honest men and down-home, unpreten-
tious, sincere women. Is it any wonder that in the country music belief system, the country should represent
an Eden-like place of fulfillment and happiness, and the
city stand for the most widely renowned Biblical seats
of vice and corruption, Sodom and Gomorrah?

Ballads in praise of the country are legion in country
music. They express all the possible images, from simplistic clichés to the profound poetry of simple observation. Dolly Parton's "Tennessee Mountain Home" describes sweet-smelling honeysuckle on the summer
wind, eagles against the clear skies, and the peaceful
melodic music of songbirds. Young people walk home
from church "laughing," "talking," stealing kisses, and
"making future plans."

Of the varied reasons for which the city is hated in
country music, I want to mention four. First, the city is
a threat to the country itself. Not only are shopping
malls and suburbs swallowing up and literally uprooting
the countryside, but the city is the source of the cold,
dirty science whose technological advances ravage and
despoil the natural grace of the green country. But in
most popular country music this creeping destruction is
less identified than quietly dreaded.

Secondly, the city is just as insensitive and cold within
its own boundaries as it is heartless and ruthless in its
dealings with the country. One well-known song called
"Detroit City" summarizes what many others express:

it tells of the country boy who wakes up hungry and alone in the cruel, unfriendly city crying, "Lord, do I want to go home!" In the last several years the biggest of cities—New York—has lured country musicians north of Nashville for lucrative concert appearances. One of the first to go there was Buck Owens, one of country music's world-traveling ambassadors. The description written by Buck himself on the back of his album is half humorous. It portrays the simple country boy in the clutches of complex and frustrating city people, all of whom have their hands out. The title song of the album, with its country metaphors and analogies, is less humorous. Buck notes ironically that New York is certainly full of hustle-bustle for a place where people have all the interpersonal space of "sardines" and as many places to go as "fleas on a puppy dog." He concludes, "I wouldn't live in New York City if they gave me the whole dang town."

The city is widely recognized as a perverter of women. When good, clean country women go into the city, they come out painted up, tarnished, and trained in the ways of the devil. Kris Kristofferson wrote about one of the silver-tongued devil men who inhabit the city and corrupt the morals of these young, innocent country women. He called it simply "The Taker." The title refers to the conniving way in which this modern city slicker would take his young victim to places and through experiences that thrilled and delighted her. Then, when he had her sufficiently intoxicated with the "splendor" of the sensational city life, he would take advantage of her, staining her soul by destroying her virtue.

Finally, the city is all that is false, artificial, pretentious, and proud, in contrast with the country's truth, natural beauty, and humble faith. A great percentage of country music fans are religious people, mostly Christian, and probably Protestant. Many know their Bibles well, and are responsive to Biblical imagery. For these people, the accusations leveled by Dolly Parton in the Porter Wagoner song "Do You Ever Hear the Robins Sing?" strike sharply at the center of the false pride of the city. "You say the view is beautiful" from your high-rise? That your artificial lawn never needs mowing? That your "buildings are so tall they almost reach heaven"? Every country music fan recognizes immediately the reference to Genesis, chapter 11: "Then they said, 'Come, let us build ourselves a city, and a tower with its top in the heavens." In contrast to hearing the robins singing in the springtime, the third line of the chorus queries: "Is all the beauty in your life just artificial things?" Perhaps country music stars are not the ones to drop that question on us like a judgment, but that doesn't lighten the burden of the denial for us city folk.

THE TRUCK DRIVER

The family is the dominant salvation motif in country music. But the individualist strain in American cultural patterns is still present in country music. Originating with the pioneer and the frontiersman, it was elevated to mythical proportions in the Western form of skilled-gunfighter-as-deliverer. Combining this tradition with the Casey Jones railroader of American folk music is the present-day truck driver. The truck driver is an ideal hero for people of lower income bracket and less than a college education. He is sometimes self-employed, always on his own. He is a rugged individual, with a reputation for being tough, aggressive, and self-made. He never wears a coat and tie, except maybe in church. He drinks, swears, and has a waitress in every truck stop. He is a man of the people, of simple needs, strong desires, and patriotic fervor. Yet he may be making up to $50,000 a year. Here is a man of means, successful, who has not sold out to the snobbery of Eastern intellectuals. Here is a man on the move, as envied for his mobility as was the railroad engineer in decades past.

Though my favorite song of this genre is "Truck Driving Man," the best-known and most characteristic truck-driving song is one recorded by Dave Dudley, called "Six Days on the Road":

I pulled outta Pittsburgh rollin' down that Eastern
　　Seaboard.
I got my diesel wound up and she's rollin' like never
　　before.
There's a speed zone ahead all right
But I don't see a cop in sight
Six days on the road and I'm gonna make it home
　　tonight.

Pushing toward home with his "ten forward gears and a Georgia overdrive," the driver confesses to what we all know is necessary: "I'm taking little white pills and my eyes are open wide." He further brags of "passing everything in sight," of being over the weight permitted by law, of not keeping his logbook up to date in his hurry to get home. He is able to dodge all the truck scales. His rig may be "a little old," he says, "but that don't mean she's slow: There's a flame from her stack

and her smoke is blowing black as coal." Now *that* is
power and speed, held in surging, driving harmony by
one tough man, willing to push himself to the limit and
unafraid of bucking regulations in the process. A special, attractive feature of this song is its family morality.
Here is the man who can have any number of women
(who's to know, right?), but who stays faithful to his
wife:

Well it seems like a month since I kissed my baby
    goodbye.
I could have a lot of women but I'm not like some
    other guys.
I could find one to hold me tight,
But I could never make believe it's all right.
Six days on the road and I'm gonna make it home
    tonight.
Earl Green and Carl Montgomery, Newkeys Music, Inc., and Tune
    Publishing Company. Copyright 1961. All rights reserved.

Tom T. Hall: A Prophetic Voice in Country Music

Generalized social commentary is more common in
country music than direct political, economic, or religious protest. Country music people are traditional pa-
triots and conservative believers. They do not accept
gracefully criticism of the political or economic systems
of this country. As a result, protest songs are rare in
country music. Few performers will touch them. There
is, however, one country singer who has sung a significant number of such songs. His name is Tom T. Hall.[35]
Hall is a college-educated songwriter, whose songs
come from the appropriate poetic combination of heart

and head. Like Bob Dylan and Tom Paxton, Hall writes about what he observes, about where he's been, about people who have touched his life with their particular brand of humanness. In addition, he is a devout Christian concerned about the state of the faith in the contemporary church, a situation often reflected in his songs.

Tom T. Hall's brand of music is rarely "causal," in the sense of advocating a form of social reform. He comes close to being a crusader only in his explicitly religious music, and then limits his criticisms to intra-Christian controversies. His targets, however, are consistently the forces opposed to what he celebrates about people in all of his music. In "One More Song for Jesus," Hall takes on institutionalized oppression and extremist perversions:

They say they're going to burn us in a not too distant
    day.
I don't think we should buy that cause it just ain't
    Jesus' way.
They say he's mean and vicious and there's nothing
    he won't do.
They must know a different Jesus than we do.

Oh, we may not live the letter of the law and live
    that true.
Judged and criticized for almost everything we do.
But they cannot stop our singing though they're
    holier than we.
Let's have one more song for Jesus if you please.

Copyrighted by Hallnote Music Co.

In his very popular "Me and Jesus," Hall challenges the intellectual leadership and superficial trappings of the established church:

We can't afford any fancy preachin'.
We can't afford any fancy church.
We can't afford any fancy singing.
But you know Jesus got a lot of poor people out
    doing his work.

Me and Jesus, we got our own thing going.
Me and Jesus, we got it all worked out.
Me and Jesus, we got our own thing going.
We don't need anybody to tell us what it's all about.
Copyrighted by Hallnote Music Co.

Hall is most appealing as a songwriter when he uses ironic twists to turn the tables on the baser instincts of his own constituency. In "Too Many Do-Goods" he sets up the listener with images that seem to be contrasting hardworking Middle Americans with welfare recipients and their bleeding-heart liberal friends. He even throws in a nasty reference to one of the favorite sons of the liberal establishment, Bob Dylan. All of this merely sets the stage for the real object of the attack, the hypocrisy of a talk-a-lot, do-nothing church:

We've got too many do-goods, and not enough
    hard-working men.
We've got too many hands out, and not enough
    lending a hand.
We've got too many people looking for the answer in
    the wind.
We've got too many do-goods and not enough
    hard-working men.

We've got clubs and committees that know all about
    wrong and right.
But I've seen too many children who starved plum
    to death on advice.

I appreciate your sympathy and I believe in
    missionary work.
But just a little bending down and picking up your
    brother wouldn't hurt.

When not calling the church for not covering its bets, Tom T. Hall occasionally indulges in social criticism, on steel mills and the people they gobble up ("The Rolling Mills of Middletown"), on society's vengeful insensitivity to the poor and outcast person ("I Washed My Face in the Morning Dew"), on the absurdity of racial prejudice ("The Man Who Hated Freckles"), on the slaughter of wild mustangs ("Running Wild"), and on suburbia ("Subdivision Blues"). But he is best known and appreciated by country music fans for his narratives about his own experiences, and the people and places they bring to life.

Some of these songs reflect his life as entertainer/superstar. In "Homecoming" he captures the awkward pauses and embarrassing excuses that have come to dominate the phone calls and visits the traveling entertainer makes to his parents' hometown, a place no longer "home" to the "star." "Spokane Motel Blues" expresses the author's frustration at being "stuck" in Spokane while Willie Nelson, Waylon Jennings, and the rest are swinging around the country where things are happening, or eating chili at Tootsie's Orchid Lounge in Nashville. Tom T. is stuck in Spokane "writing a song" —without even a Dolly Parton tape to keep him company! In what I suspect is a personal rather than a general warning, Hall sings of one of the musician's deadliest pitfalls:

Joe, don't let your music kill you.
It's the thing that's supposed to fill you.
It's the thing that's supposed to make you happy.
Taking pills and drinking whiskey.
Picking can be mighty risky.
Joe, don't let your music kill you, nobody cares.

In a typical mixture of cold, ironic observation—sounding elitist and a put-down—and empathetic feeling for his audience, Tom T. pours forth images of the concert tour and bourbon in the same early-morning song:

We were drinking too much yesterday,
Nobody's ever told us what's enough.
The ones we should have prayed for more than
    likely
Were the ones we had to cuss.
They applauded while we killed ourselves
But angels don't have bourbon on their breath.
The thing that keeps us going is the
Good folks in the last hard town we met.

They came to see the people that they thought we
    were
And never changed their minds.
They explained away the difference cause the
Folks that love a picker can be blind.
They misunderstood the words but understood
That our intentions were the best.
The thing that keeps us going is the
Good folks in the last hard town we met.

The people Hall writes about are the normally unnoticed and often "undesirable" members of the human community: the alcoholic wife of a friend; "Ravishing

Ruby" the truck-stop waitress biding her time while awaiting the return of "smiling Jack," her mythical father; Clayton Delaney, the wine-drinking, guitar-picking itinerant of Hall's boyhood hometown; a "Shoeshine Man" with pride in the work that he does; a small-town sheriff, unimpressed by who Hall is, who keeps him locked in the local jail for a week for speeding—where one could come to relish "hot baloney, eggs and gravy"; a slick, big-time pool shark who takes the small-time hustler to the cleaners. None has been more popular than Hall's tale about the opinions of a sixty-five-year-old, gray-haired, black custodian who bent Hall's ear in the lounge of a Miami hotel.

> I was sitting in Miami pouring blended whiskey
>   down
> When this old, gray black gentleman was
>   cleaning up the lounge.
> There wasn't anyone around 'cept this old man and
>   me.
> The guy who ran the bar was watching "Ironsides"
>   on TV.
> Uninvited he sat down and opened up his mind,
> On old dogs and children, and watermelon wine.
>   Copyrighted by Hallnote Music Co.

After detailing the delights of watermelon wine, and discounting the concerns of women and friends, the old man claims that only three things in this world are "worth a solitary dime"—old dogs, children, and watermelon wine. Sharply contrasting with the philosophy of Merle Haggard's "Branded," which still assumes the normal standards of American society by which forgiveness must be earned, and thus merited, Hall tells us the final words of the old man's thoughts:

Old dogs care about you even when you make
    mistakes.
God bless little children while they're still too young
    to hate.
When he moved away I found my pen and copied
    down that line,
About old dogs and children, and watermelon wine.

Here is a value from the Christian belief system, one antithetical to what is normally represented in the American belief system. From the mouth of one who has been through the American system comes a condemnation of it—a condemnation in the form of an alternative. A Christian who is listening for God's presence can scarcely miss it here.

5

Popular Magazines:
INSTRUCTION MANUALS
OF MALE AND FEMALE IDENTITY

One woman, overheard at a party, said to another, "I've been my father's daughter, my husband's wife, and Bill's girl friend. I think it's about time I tried being me for a while." The task of "being me" occupies substantial portions of the waking hours of the average individual. Americans embrace all kinds of communal fulfillment, from nuclear family to national association, from the two-by-twoing of the mating-dating ritual to massive protest rallies and national conventions. Yet from the far right to the radical left in the American political spectrum, a fierce and assertive individualism characterizes the American self-image: I am "me" *before* I am "me and you" or "us."

The dominant belief system appearing in American popular culture affirms the family or some other form of communal organization as the place of human fulfillment. Correspondingly, it represents the problems of life as due to some break in communal relations. Films, television, country music, detective fiction, all provide ample illustrations to demonstrate this point. But we noted above (in Chapter 2) that a subdominant set of values centering on individual fulfillment surfaces in the style of life of the individualist deliverer-hero who we believe can save our community from evil interlopers. We walk, talk, slouch, and grimace like these larger-than-life images of *real* "man." These deliverer figures embody an image of fulfilled human individualism that reduces our ordinary mortal coping to shadowy inferiority. "Cyclops," writing in the Sunday *New York Times,* puts it well:

I blame Robert Redford. In agreeing to play the part of Bob Woodward in "All the President's Men," he transformed the investigative reporter from a suspicious drudge into a matinee idol, a Tarzan with a typewriter. Who among us could go on living an ordinary life after Robert Redford has portrayed us on the screen? We are so much less than he is. It would be like setting up permanent residence in a discrepancy.[36]

Few Americans will have this "problem"; but who among us does not feel trapped in that "discrepancy"? Here popular magazines meet us where we live. Unlike other popular culture media, popular magazines devote their entire attention to merchandising styles of individual fulfillment. If you want a quick assessment of a person's self-image, take note what magazines line the living room coffee table or the bedroom nightstand. Popular magazines tell us how to cultivate and harvest the self-image we feel growing within us.

From among the hundreds of periodicals one might analyze, these few to which we now turn fall under one or the other of two broad categories: increasingly influential, urban images of maleness and/or femaleness; or decreasingly influential, more traditional American male and female self-images. Under the first category we will examine *Ladies' Home Journal, Cosmopolitan,* and *Ms.* for images of female individuality, and *Playboy* for a view of fulfilled male humanness. The second category includes observations on maleness as defined by such magazines as *Outdoor Life, Field & Stream, Argosy, True,* and self-understandings of femaleness found in romance magazines.

IMAGES INCREASING IN INFLUENCE

Three Views of Being a Woman in America: *Ladies' Home Journal, Cosmopolitan,* and *Ms.*

The fulfilled woman as understood by *Ladies' Home Journal* is the homemaker/wife. Her individuality stays hidden behind her function as enabler in the family. Fulfillment as an individual comes in doing things for others, specifically for her husband and children. This woman operates an efficient home, though as a sacrificial figure, living not her own separate life, but a life identified with her home and family.

The "sacrificial" image bears elaboration. The individuality of this woman realizes itself in her house and her children. She does not so much give up being a distinctly unique individual as she projects her "self" into extensions of herself. Her "dresses" are draperies and furniture, her "cosmetics" decorative paints and bric-a-brac. The television commercial in which the bridge club members arrive to immediately wrinkle their noses at the "fishy odor" of the house implicitly accuses the housewife of "BO." This woman's social identity is her house and her children. In this sense, she sacrifices her individuality.

As enabler of the smoothly operating family, the

homemaker/wife accepts a passive social role. The male dominates, in the sense that the female lives *for* the male. Being naturally more aggressive, he protects the home, employing his crafty, skilled ways with the "world outside" to finance its operation. He forages while she holds down the fort. She becomes representative of stability, laced with naïveté—sweetness and compassion integrated with innocence. He must constantly do battle with a challenging, changing, hostile environment. It is not uncommon for the corrosiveness of working outside the home to wear him down with frustrations and pressures like a cancerous disease. A home situation of healing grace, of quiet and refuge, is the homemaker/wife's responsibility. In providing this, her passivity is a virtue—more, a basic strength.

Ladies' Home Journal caters to images that reinforce the woman as homemaker/wife. Baking bread and making your own clothes represent the professional skills of homemaking. Here traditional secrets of the "profession" of homemaker are handed down from Grandmother, via *Ladies' Home Journal,* to you. Articles speaking to the homemaker/wife as concerned mother abound, as do advertisements appealing to the reader who really cares about her child's dental hygiene. Indicative of the extensive care given by the *Journal* and like magazines to the sacrificial image of the homemaker/wife is a pictorial article from a few years back entitled "Fathers and Daughters." Over the caption "A son's a son until he takes a wife . . . But a daughter's a daughter for all of her life" are pictures of seven celebrities and their daughters. Every homemaker/wife wants to be the wife/mother that her own father would have wanted. The homemaker/wife/

mother role partially fulfills a fantasy of that wish. Not every woman's father is a celebrity, except of course in her own eyes. But that hardly presents a problem for this article. The author makes the transition to the image-expectations of her reader in the first two short paragraphs of the story:

The right kind of relationship between a father and daughter is especially vital to the daughter, says psychiatrist Theodore Isaac Rubin. "It is of inestimable importance because a father is the first man in a girl's life and he invariably has a profound effect on how she will relate to men throughout her life." . . . The daughters of celebrity fathers often experience special problems: they must share daddy with the rest of the world, and their own achievements sometimes suffer by comparison. But at heart, celebrity fathers are no different from other fathers—whether they are presidents, governors, movie stars or sports figures.[37]

A perusal of the advertisements of the *Journal* supports this analysis of the homemaker/wife image. Approximately 60 percent of the ads concern the purchase and preparation of food and the interior design or improvement of the home. Virtually no advertisements for clothing appear in the *Journal,* with the exception of nylon ads. Twenty percent of the ads do offer various kinds of makeup and perfume, and 13 percent or so deal with cigarettes or liquor. Interestingly, more ads for aspirin or pain-relief medicines appear in the *Journal* than in *Cosmopolitan* or *Ms.*

Health-related articles and ads focus mainly upon faces growing inevitably older and hands that are cracked or chapped from constant immersion in dishwater or scrub bucket. Of other health problems, cancer engages the most attention, but is apt to be dealt with vicariously through the world of celebrities: "Shirley Temple's Breast Cancer," "Hubert Humphrey, My Fight Against Cancer."

Understandably, magazines like the *Journal* do not feature travel ads or articles. More common would be the suggestion that the homemaker bring faraway places into her home: "Bring the Orient Into Your Bedroom." Encouraged here is redecoration, rather than slipping a Chinese kung-fu fighter in the bedroom window.

Since this analysis depends partially on the contrast of the *Journal* image with the images projected by *Cosmopolitan* and *Ms.*, one striking feature of the *Journal* homemaker/wife/mother person should be remembered. The proffered image of fulfilled womanhood relates individuality in its fullness to a form of community, in this case the family. No person is homemaker, wife, or mother in isolation. To be a fulfilled individual woman is to be a member, functionally integrated, of a community—however small the social unit. Individuality is defined *in terms of* community.

Cosmopolitan is the most expertly packaged belief system available in manual form, with the possible exception of *Playboy* magazine. Every page offers direction or advice toward attaining the "Cosmo Girl" image, as represented on the cover of each monthly issue. Called by critics a "masscult update of the 'Kama Sutra' as interpreted by Baby Snooks,"[38] *Cosmopolitan* has ridden the liberated philosophy of editor Helen Gurley Brown to over two million in circulation, 90 percent of which is newsstand sales! While moralists think up catchy one-line put-downs, the Brown and company

Cosmo Girl image has become a major option for American women.

The Cosmo Girl is fundamentally a sexual creature, a sensuous, pleasure-seeking, man-oriented woman. Complete and fulfilled womanhood for the Cosmo Girl image includes a man, specifically a man with whom one can experience pleasure, or more explicitly, sexual pleasure. As Helen Gurley Brown says, the Cosmo Girl "loves men and doesn't feel complete or even *alive* unless she has one." All men are fair game, even married men. As Ms. Brown says, "There simply isn't enough product to go around." Correspondingly, the magazine features regular articles on the single woman–married man affair, such as, "Will Your Married Lover Ever Leave His Wife?" The designs of the Cosmo Girl do not, however, necessarily include marriage, whatever the level of the sexual relationship. Sexual relations with a man can be liberating, and are not conditioned by future intent or even the rakish reputation of the man:

The first Casanova I was involved with wasn't much to look at; the second, though handsome, was unsophisticated; and the third was a failure in his career. . . . Still, despite their limitations, these three lovers taught me a lot about relating pleasurably to men. They were so good to be with that I simply forgot to play games, or to hide behind a witty, sophisticated mask. I had fun instead! . . . One of these men, by the way, was married, and he adored his wife, just as he did every other woman he met. And this brings me to one last point about Casanovas: they make wonderful companions and bed partners, but you must never never make the mistake of marrying one. . . . He is a joy, a treasure and a sexual marvel, but emotionally, he's a dropout! Don't plan to call him at 3:00 A.M. with problems. . . . This is Casanova's only fault, however, and it's one that for the length of a brief, lovely affair, at least, you may want to *forgive.* [39]

The antithesis of the Cosmo Girl is the homemaker/wife/mother of *Ladies' Home Journal.* Professional housewives appear uptight and jealous in *Cosmopolitan.* They are baby factories who tie down men, while showing their weakness by being totally dependent on their husbands. As Helen Gurley Brown says: "I know I've been able to do what I've done because I have no children . . . but women don't have to have more children. They could get it together but they don't." As a defense against being trapped in the destructive homemaker/wife/mother image, the Cosmo ethic is strict—all women should work outside the home and express themselves in their work. Every woman should be self-supporting financially.

The *Journal* is replete with children, in articles, columns, ads. In vivid contrast, children have no place in the pages of *Cosmopolitan.* Moreover, as the above quote may indicate, in the Cosmo world view children and housewives come in one package. Not unexpectedly, then, *Cosmopolitan* tends to take a negative view of the presence of children in one's life. For example, one issue featured a story entitled, "The Beginning of the End of Sex: The First Baby." In four double-columned pages, only three to four sentences express sentiments like "A child expands you and your capacity to love," or confess that having a child is "worth what you have to give up in your sex life and your life in general." The rest of the article sounds more like the following summary:

Obsession, fatigue, loss of sensuality, loss of privacy, economic pressures, illness, loss of spontaneity. If it seems as though I am stacking the cards, I am not. And if your response is, how do people manage? the answer is, many don't. The divorce rate is ghastly and I wouldn't want to guess at the happy marriage rate. . . . If having a baby affects your sex life, undermines your privacy, diminishes romance and spontaneity, and sets in motion pressures unlike any your marriage has known, why in the world have a child? Many people aren't. The right not to have children is being asserted by more and more couples. And many people shouldn't.[40]

The advertisements in *Cosmopolitan* reveal the same contrast with the *Journal*. *Cosmo* carries no food ads, and very few references to interior design or homemaking. *Cosmopolitan* ads tell the neophyte how to look stylish or smell good. Over 70 percent of the ads deal explicitly with fashion or makeup, 20 percent with cigarettes or booze, and 7 percent with feminine odor (as opposed to a fraction of a percentage in the *Journal*).

Since the Cosmo Girl is solely her own person, each issue of the magazine features at least one travel article, such as carnivals in Rio and luxury-liner trips. The sections dealing with health emphasize fitness and familiarity with your body. Love your body, know it, keep it in shape, that's the Cosmo Girl's motto. Pleasure requires a healthy body and a free mind.

While the female image in the *Journal* finds individual fulfillment in terms of others (specifically, the family), the Cosmo Girl as an ideal is totally self-contained, self-supporting, completely realized in herself alone.

Though her nirvana includes a man, the Cosmo Girl has her choice of many, none of whom is more essential to her fulfillment than any other.

The cover of *Ladies' Home Journal* features one of two possibilities each issue: either a whole or partial family (for example, sisters); or a "suburban"-looking female celebrity as a lead-in to a story about her family life. *Cosmopolitan*'s cover trademark is the sultry seductress the magazine is training its devotees to become.

Not unexpectedly the monthly cover of *Ms.* presents its own version of fulfilled individual womanhood. *Ms.* magazine offers Bella Abzug, Katharine Graham, or Ingrid Bergman, women known for their achievements outside the kitchen and the bedroom, in the "man's world" of business, entertainment, education, politics.

Like the Cosmo Girl, the *Ms.* woman supports herself. Unlike the Cosmo Girl, fulfillment for the *Ms.* woman does not necessarily include a man. The Cosmo Girl works so she may maintain her free-lancing sexual activities, which are the actual source of her fulfillment. The *Ms.* woman finds the fulfilled life in her profession. She may choose sex, or choose not to have it. In any case, sex is tangential to complete personhood. And, if the *Ms.* woman chooses a sexual relationship, she may choose either male or female as her partner—an unthinkable option for the Cosmo Girl.

Ms. assumes that its reader not only has an intelligent mind, but likes to use it. A profile of *Ms.* readership bears out that assumption.[41] Twice as many attended college as Cosmo readers, and a third hold advanced degrees. Half of its readers earn over $10,000 a year. A survey of other magazines read by *Ms.* followers placed such periodicals as *Psychology Today, Saturday Review World,* and *Intellectual Digest* as strong preferences, while only 5 percent admitted to regular reading of *Cosmopolitan.*

The actively involved, professional-woman-as-person image sold by *Ms.* marks the advertisements. In the *Journal,* ads for food and interior home design dominate; in *Cosmopolitan* clothing and makeup ads far outnumber any other type. In *Ms.* some of these ads can be found, but bracketed by ads for ecology, Diners Club cards, Merrill Lynch, and *Harper's Magazine.*

Two other characteristics of *Ms.* magazine relate it to the *Journal* and sharply distinguish it from *Cosmopolitan.* First, like the homemaker/wife/mother of the *Journal,* whose individual fulfillment essentially includes a community, the *Ms.* woman's image of full personhood is communal. The *Ms.* woman has a strong sense of sisterhood, and a fiercely defensive posture at the least sign of male intruders or critics. As a result, *Ms.* has often been accused of taking a sexist, anti-male stance. Secondly, *Ms.* and the *Ladies' Home Journal* both affirm children. *Ms.* regularly features articles on children, and includes ads in which children appear prominently. The magazine is known for having produced the record and television show "Free to Be You and Me," probably the most creative and innovative, nonpatronizing approach to concern for the world of children ever presented in the media.

Even more indicative of the *Ms.* concern for the meaning and significance of children in human adult fulfillment is the way the magazine often handles the tricky intra-movement debate on the question "Must we be childless to be free?" The Cosmo Girl would say

"Yes!" But note what Ellen Willis writes in *Ms.*, a position that seems representative of the magazine:

There is an obvious arrogance in the assumption of some of the militantly childless . . . that their way of life is more desirable than other people's. . . . But their position is also arrogant in a more insidious and ultimately more harmful way: they seem to regard the worst aspects of motherhood not as oppressive conditions that should be alleviated but as intrinsic disadvantages that should be avoided by people with smarts. . . . Far from being in any sense feminist, this attitude is thoroughly conservative. . . . This view misses the essential point: that our system of child-rearing lays on mothers an enormous responsibility that by rights should be shared by fathers and the community at large. Just as many mothers resent this inequitable burden, I resent the fact that I can't have children unless I'm willing to assume it. Of course I'm happy to have a choice, as I might not have had 20 years ago. But the choice is scarcely "free." For me, as for the rebellious mother, the answer is political change. . . . Again, the fundamental issue is not which choice we make, but why each choice must cost us part of our humanity. As individuals, we ask, "Is it worth the cost?" As a movement, we must ask, "Why is it always we who have to pay?"[42]

One final index of the differences in the images of womanhood offered by these three magazines is a comparison of the same advertisement in two different magazines. A Honda Civic (a small car) ad in *Cosmopolitan* is a two-page layout. The page on the left—the one the reader comes across first—shows a young man standing beside a Honda Civic under a list of fifteen reasons he prefers the car. But the man is not looking at the reader; rather, he is gazing across the center crease at the right-hand page and scratching his head in bewilderment. On the right-hand page a young woman in sporty clothes, wearing a smug smile of self-satisfaction, stands beside a Honda Civic under the same list of fifteen reasons *she* prefers to drive the car. She can like the car for the same reasons any man can! So there! In *Ms.* the Honda Civic is presented by itself, under the caption, "We don't make a woman's car." Honda makes a car for any person to drive, not one that is complicated (for a man) and one that is simple (for a woman).

A Butterick (Instant Fashion patterns) ad in *Cosmopolitan* and the same company's ad in *Ms.* use the identical layout and word-for-word the very same text (with the exception that the *Ms.* ad is for a leisure fall jump suit, and the *Cosmo* ad is for an evening gown). What is different is the picture: the *Ms.* model in the jump suit is alone; the *Cosmopolitan* model in the evening gown is shown with her adoring man, standing just behind her, hand softly on her arm, nose and mouth nuzzling her hair.

Finally, an ad for Samsonite luggage ("A New Bag Named Sam") in the *Journal* shows Winnie and Arnold Palmer packing and ready to take off together in Arnie's private jet. The same company's ad in *Cosmopolitan* portrays a woman embracing a man in an airport hallway, presumably having just flown in to meet him. Complementing the picture's impression that she is the mobile one—coming to visit him—and adding to the inference that this rendezvous is an affair (rather than a meeting of husband and wife, or business) is the caption over the ad: "What sticks close, never intrudes and keeps all your deepest secrets? A Bag Named Sam."

The *Playboy* **Male**[43]

The image of fulfilled male individuality presented in completely packaged form by *Playboy* magazine includes the following characteristics: affluent, intelligent, urbane, discriminating in taste, stylish in dress and travel, interested in sports of all kinds, as both spectator and participant, philosophically naturalistic and relativistic, and politically libertarian rightest.[44] But the cornerstone of this massive structure is a modern, hedonistic version of the cool, imperturbable, sophisticated deliverer-hero of the Western form. Why is the Western hero so cool? Why is he always so unruffled? Because, unlike the rest of us, he is never taken by surprise in any situation. The knowledge and wisdom by which he sizes up every possibility before it occurs is the key to his awesome presence and powerful personality. The *Playboy* male binds all his character elements together with a similar, singular quality. He has the requisite knowledge of all the contingent possibilities and ingredients of any and all social situations, so that he feels perfectly at home in every setting and at any event. This expertise is nothing in itself; it is purely and simply the means to a style of life, to an image of complete male fulfillment. It is a kind of knowledge most appropriately dubbed "sophistication."

The style has always been visually represented throughout the magazine. The formally attired *Playboy* Rabbit with his smug smile, his eyes half closed in casual boredom while surrounded by beautiful women, fast sports cars, and exotic beaches, symbolizes this life-relation. The men in the ads are cool, detached, elite, impeccably dressed. They exude arrogance, without seeming aristocratic. Each one is attended by a beautiful woman, fashionably windblown, pliant, and adoringly draped around the irresistible object of her attention, this *Playboy* man. Lest anyone miss the point, the magazine includes with each issue not only a picture of this man, who makes a woman spin around to get a second look, but a brief description as well. To the question, "What kind of a man reads *Playboy?*" the following responses are offered:

A man who has an appreciation not only for fine art but for the fine art of living as well . . . he exercises taste and discrimination.

A man who knows exactly what he's after and where he'll find it. . . . But whether he's exploring new waters or speculating in stocks, he relies on expertise, not luck.

A man with a sense of style. One who'll go out of his way to find attire that expresses his individual personality.

This informal instruction is more than complemented by the magazine's direct and indirect formal advice to aspiring males. Indirect instruction fills the record, book, and film review sections, bringing us continually up-to-date on the "in" vocalist, band, novelist, or director. "Playboy After Hours" tunes the reader to the latest thing everyone is talking about. "Playboy Forum" wages endless assaults on those political, social, and religious institutions which attempt to legislate morality by enforcing their standards on everybody else. The *Playboy* male vehemently protests the prosecution of victimless crimes, particularly those pertaining to sexual activities in private places, but also including private consumption of drugs. He is greatly concerned about snooping governmental agencies. The style and tone of the "Playboy Forum" continually reflects editor Hugh Hefner's well-known religious prejudice, that obsolete theological doctrine is the source of repressive sexual legislation. The cool and detached image of the *Playboy* male, however, precludes much involvement in political causes.

Direct instruction is plentiful and necessarily relevant. *Playboy* tells its neophyte sophisticate what to wear and how it wear it, what cars to drive, what to eat and what to wash it down with, where to go for exciting vacations, how to throw successful parties, and so on. For those who still have questions, there is the "Playboy Advisor," interspersing responses to questions about appropriate attire and wines with advice on the physical and emotional problems of male-female sexual sports.

Letters to the editor strongly reinforce those hesitant to believe that following the leader will result in the promised fulfillment. They show that *high status professionals* in American society not only read *Playboy,* they approve. If ministers, senators, professors of anthropology, psychologists, administrative heads of national organizations of all shapes and sizes think *Playboy* is all right, it must be all right. Travel articles provide vicarious fulfillment for the timid and the trapped. You can visit small restaurants in Capri and luxuriant coral reefs in the South Pacific without ever leaving your living room chair.

The Playmate, who folds out in the center of each issue, is the prize. There she stands, staring directly at you, two cigarettes burning in the ashtray, undressing or stepping out of the shower—*for you.* This Playmate is not your typical promiscuous dumb bunny. She epitomizes the woman the *Playboy* man seeks for himself. The women in *Playboy* are not sex objects merely, though it may seem that they are. The Playmate is shown in informal pictures flipping pancakes with her parents (who approve of the pinup), joking with girl friends, on dates formal and informal. She is the girl next door, healthy, uninhibited, and fully rounded— and not only physically. The Playmate may be in a Ph.D. program at Berkeley, in a chess tournament in the French Alps, singing part-time in a coffeehouse, skiing in the Rockies, and generally just a fun girl. She is an interesting, intelligent woman who enjoys sex, and who cannot resist the fully complete *Playboy* image when he wafts by. She is a decent, involved, respectable girl, who is willing and waiting for a cool, imperturbable *Playboy* man to wrap herself around.

Two Images Decreasing in Influence

The Romance Magazine: Female as Victim[45]

Helen Gurley Brown has said that *Cosmopolitan* is dedicated to reversing the image of the female presented by the soap opera and the romance magazine. Cosmo promises that "you can become the sexual aggressor, have a great time, and not feel guilty afterward: you can transform yourself from victimized virgin to sultry seductress." Whether or not *Cosmopolitan* has "turned the tide," the romance magazine continues to sell widely, supporting the inference that a sharply different concept of being a woman is still abroad in America.

Over thirty different magazines of this type are still

published, with names as well known as *True Confessions,* as ungarnished as *Revealing Romances,* and as cover-all as *True Modern Love Confessions.* Readership as recently as 1970 was estimated at over thirteen million. The major part of these readers are young, married, lower-middle-class and lower-class housewives and preteen girls; the major market is the American Midwest.

The woman of the romance magazine has been sexually victimized. The dream world of sexual fantasy and the lived-in world of sexual reality are starkly dissimilar. Somewhere between the two, the meaningful, satisfying life of stable, loving interpersonal relations has been disrupted, distorted, or all but destroyed. Life has overwhelmed this woman. Illicit sexual experience has somehow degenerated the love for which she yearned.

In romance magazine stories the narrator—usually a young woman eighteen to twenty-five years of age—describes a sexual experience or situation that has reduced her home and family life to chaos. She was raped by her father, she is involved in a degrading affair with a man who doesn't love her, she is engaged to marry a man she doesn't love while having overwhelming sexual fantasies about her best friend's fiancé. Yet the stories are not so much about the sexual causes as about the traumatic personal guilt and anxiety suffered by the heroine. About a quarter of the stories end in devastating judgment on the woman. Even though she was not actively at fault, but only yielded briefly to temptation, or was overwhelmed by the circumstances, still she suffers the stain of illicit sex. Another 25 percent show that love and understanding between family members can make everything all right and heal the gaping wounds of guilt and shame. The majority of the stories end in ambiguity, holding out the possibility of restored interpersonal relations and renewed love, while witnessing to the indelible marks of guilt.

Romance magazines, in spite of their preoccupation with sexual events, are laced with traditional American moral values. Though intercourse and kissing are featured parts of these stories about 60 to 70 percent of the time, oral-genital sex is absolutely taboo, heavy petting is rarely mentioned, and extramarital sex is the smallest source of these story lines. The covers of the magazines promise vicarious illicit thrills, but the stories themselves swiftly reinforce the belief that people who actually do these things have their lives reduced to shambles by them. Romance magazines are bastions of the public morality. Sex is volatile and dangerous, and must be carefully contained within certain prescribed rules and regulations. The major threat to the home and family is sexual exploitation, taking rather than giving, and women are mainly the victims. The same conscious anxiety is raised as when the outlaw threatens the schoolmarm/rancher's daughter of the Western: sexual exploitation of the homemaker/wife/mother is equivalent to the rape of Western civilization.

The woman who reads the romance magazine already holds the values reinforced therein, but secretly craves the thrill of defying her own cloistered existence. Her lust-fear attraction to illicit sexuality sells the magazines. They pander to the lust while protecting their reader's vicarious participation with strong moral sanctions. The great percentage of advertisements proffer ways to become a more sexually alluring woman—bust development, weight loss, beauty aids, fashions. Most of these readers know that such tampering will not result in the major life transformation they fantasize. So a great many more ads offer quick ways to improve the life situation itself: loans, medicine, indeed even religion.

Male Chauvinism, Machismo Style [46]

In the barbershops of Middle America, the final outposts of predominantly male presence, women's magazines are nonexistent and *Playboy* is rarely found. But another type of men's magazine abounds. Popular titles include *True* ("For Today's Active Man"), *Argosy* ("Man's World of Adventure"), *Field & Stream, Hunting & Fishing, Guns & Ammo,* and *Outdoor Life.* Their readers are *real* men, the kind Teddy Roosevelt would have admired. They have bumper stickers on their pickup trucks that read "Guns don't kill people; People kill people." They prefer to associate with other men, rather than with women. They find exhilaration and "life's gusto" (you only go around once, you know) in pitting strength and skill, courage and endurance, against nature itself. They are Burt Reynolds in the film *Deliverance.*

These men are all married and have their fill of domesticity at home, which is what women represent. Women, as in the classic American belief system, tie men down, make them civilized, responsible citizens. Thus, when these men have time free from their tedious jobs, the last thing they want is to sit at home or go to the P.T.A. meeting. You will find little mention of home, wife, family, or children in these magazines. Women sometimes appear as sex objects in the advertisements, but they are as nonessential to fulfillment of this male image as are men to the *Ms.* woman. Male camaraderie *is* essential, however, a perspective that this view of being male has in common with the *Ms.* version of being female. No woman can appreciate sitting in a tree for eight hours waiting for a deer to come by, but sportsmen can.

The heroic male of these magazines is an individual who combines a gutsy willpower with highly developed outdoor skills to meet some supreme natural challenge and conquer it. The magazine features true stories of great adventures, pages of advertisements offering shortcuts to building the body strength necessary to endure such adventures, and all the necessary equipment and gear one would need to succeed. The equipment advertised promises in its technical superiority to make up for the edge the original adventurer has in native ability and years of practical experience.

For those men who feel all the more suffocated by their own plight when they read of the exploits of these *real* men, many of the ads offer appealing options: "Be an explosives expert," "Be a detective," "Be a bartender." Yet other portions of the magazines testify to a far deeper malaise in these men's lives than such self-help cures can remedy. Exposé articles, critical of large organizations such as the American Medical Association or the National Association of Manufacturers, are common. Government and legal agencies that threaten individual freedoms are also criticized. The infiltration of business by crime syndicates and policemen on the take may be subjects of attention. Not only do such articles play to an already threatened and hostile audience, but they all claim to be telling the full or true story, implying that newspaper and main-line newsmagazine coverage of these groups is full of half-truths and can't be trusted. (Spiro Agnew, where are you?) Actually, the claimed exposés are little more than summaries of widely known facts, concluded with questions suggesting that the public has not been given the full story.

Complementing these "who can you trust" articles are purportedly scientific reports on UFO's, demon possession, cryogenics (freezing people for long storage), astrological systems for winning on the horses, psychic powers that cause physical objects to move, and so on. The fantasized wish to circumvent presently closed social channels to the fulfilled life promotes confidence in such reports. Not unexpectedly, these magazines carry get-rich-quick ads, such as "Secrets of a Professional Gambler," "Send for the Bet-o-meter to Beat the Horses," "I made $35,000 in Just One Day at Home in Bed with the Flu," "Find buried treasure with powerful electronic detector," "Songs and Poems Needed," and "How to Publish a Book."

The outdoor life is basically an escape existence, to which only a small portion of one's lifetime can be devoted. Tedious, unsatisfying jobs and the unrelenting pressures of family time and financial responsibilities plague the majority of waking hours. Hope in a hopeless situation can be offered only by get-rich-quick fantasies and the belief that "they," society's institutions, are somehow the real cause of the problem.

COMPARISONS AND CONTRASTS

Even in this selective sampling, obvious comparisons beg our attention. Of these, we will attempt two kinds: first, some comparisons on subjects common to all the magazines; second, a glance at trends inferred from the shift in popularity from romance and barbershop magazines to such as *Cosmopolitan, Playboy,* and *Ms.*

Four of the magazines link individual fulfillment to some form of community. *Ladies' Home Journal* and the romance magazines stress the family. The barbershop magazines and *Ms.* prefer communities of the same sex as the individual. From our study of the Western form, we recognize the male comradeship of the barbershop magazines as essentially that of the outlaw group. Both are external to the community and both threaten the centrality of the family as the base community. Such male camaraderie is a flight from the suffocation of family life. The sisterhood community of *Ms.* poses a like threat. Its membership breaches institutionally established women's groups such as sewing circles. *Cosmopolitan* and *Playboy* exclude any form of community as essential to the full humanity of the individual.

What about relationships with a single member of the opposite sex? Here a clear division appears. Romance magazines, where the woman is seen as victim, often portray the man as victimizer. Men are part of the source of the problem. Similarly in the barbershop magazines, women play the role delineated in the Western, domesticator of the male. As wives, they are part of the source of the problem that these magazines address. On the other hand, *Ladies' Home Journal, Cos-*

mopolitan, and *Playboy* all require a member of the
opposite sex for fulfillment, as husband or sexual partner. The *Ms.* woman can take him or leave him, though
clearly the more strident arguments favor the latter.

Sexual relations as a part of fulfilled individual life is
another subject of some disagreement. In the romance
magazine, sex is part of the source of the problem. Barbershop magazines totally repress the subject by direct-
ing natural energies into other channels—strenuously
exhausting outdoor adventures and/or shooting one's
gun at targets less complex than females. In contrast to
this, *Cosmopolitan* and *Playboy* consider sexual experience an acceptable part of the *Ladies' Home Journal*
family world, but in the *Journal* context they don't talk
much about it. The *Ms.* woman enjoys sex, and doesn't
hesitate to talk about it, but certainly considers it grossly
overrated as a source of fulfilled personal identity.

What kind of knowledge (or informed ability) is requisite for the fulfilled life? The *Ladies' Home Journal*
wife/homemaker needs to know a thousand little technical skills, mostly "how to" kinds of knowledge. The
barbershop magazines and *Cosmopolitan* also stress
certain special skills as necessary to the fulfilled life. In
Cosmopolitan, these skills are primarily sexual—whatever is necessary to create irresistible exotic sensuality
and the social gamesmanship in which to best display it.
Barbershop magazines laud the survival skills of the
rugged outdoorsman, emphasizing most the expertise
of hunting and fishing. *Playboy,* on the other hand,
preaches social sophistication, the inner cool developed
by attention to preparedness for every social occasion.
This knowledge is more style-oriented than skill-ori-
ented. All the various bits of necessary information are

means to maintaining the fully self-contained, imperturbable individual. *Ms.* magazine demands a broad social awareness, particularly a sensitivity to the manipulation of role models in the culture. The victimized woman of the romance magazine is a creature of traditional morality—she already *knows* right from wrong. Knowledge doesn't help her. Circumstances are overwhelming, and knowledge cannot stem their destructive tide. Also the barbershop magazines point to the trapped feeling of general helplessness before life's overwhelming problems. Special skills are not helpful in dealing with these greater problems.

Part of the shift in the American cultural search for the self-image of the fulfilled individual is reflected here. *Ladies' Home Journal, Cosmo, Playboy,* and *Ms.* exude a confidence based in an optimistic view of the human situation. For these magazines, life is malleable —knowledge can change your life situation for the better. Social roles are not frozen. If you don't like where you are, *you* can change your own location, professionally, financially, geographically. The romance and barbershop magazines view Creation as a fixed, fallen world, where suffering must be endured. Human knowledge can in no way effect changes in such a world. *Ladies' Home Journal* straddles this issue, mixing optimistic self-improvement incentives with limited frontiers like "home" and overwhelming health problems.

Changing attitudes toward sex and sexuality also highlight the shifting of image priorities from romance and barbershop magazines to *Ms., Playboy, Cosmopolitan,* and the *Journal.* Relations between the sexes directly caused all our problems (romance magazines) or had to be repressed and redirected (barbershop magazines) to sustain traditional moral values in life outside the home. In both cases, sex meant trouble. In *Cosmo* and *Playboy,* sexual relations are central to human fulfillment. Far from being the cause of suffering, degeneration and distress, sex is the source of interpersonal wholeness, and thus of individual fulfillment. Neither the *Journal* nor *Ms.* considers sex as central to individual fulfillment, but both have positive attitudes toward it.

What about the importance of community sharing to individual fulfillment? Here indicators predict a possible trouble spot. In the romance and barbershop magazines, individual fulfillment included community participation. The former revered the family; the latter sought male comradeship. *Ladies' Home Journal,* an older magazine, has always supported the family as the community in which individual female lives could be complete. It continues that emphasis to the present day. *Ms.* introduces a newer form of community involvement, sisterhood. *Cosmopolitan* and *Playboy,* reflecting perhaps the anonymity of urban life and the disposable nature of human relationships, reject community for self-supporting autonomy. A woman who finds the *Cosmopolitan* image lonely and unfulfilling can always find community in the *Ms.* or *Journal* alternatives. But the shift from the proffered male comradeship of the barbershop magazines to the self-supporting, isolated *Playboy* man is a radical one. Perhaps the vicarious experience of male camaraderie in spectator sports will compensate. Perhaps not. Perhaps community is not essential to fulfilled individual life. Perhaps.

6

Television:
CULTURAL RELIGION
AT FAMILY WORSHIP

Lieutenant Columbo stands ankle-deep in the carpet of the foyer. One hand is on the hard-boiled egg in his pocket. The other arm clutches his beagle who was kicked out of dog-training school for demoralizing the other dogs. The floor is carpeted wall-to-wall, but the foyer could be Grand Central Station. Columbo is awed, as usual. The butler, still eyeing the waiting police lieutenant with disdainful skepticism, returns with his "master," the impeccably dressed, cool and elite surgeon (or is he a lawyer or international chess champion?), whom we have all just watched murder his brother (or was it his uncle? his nephew?) with style and grace. I wiggle in my chair, gleefully anticipating the first of what I know will be a series of encounters between hero and villain. As usual, this slick, know-it-all professional is rich and arrogant. He will underestimate Columbo's intelligence and perseverance. Columbo looks like a warmed-over derelict from society's lower echelons, certain to be dismissed as a dumb, nonperson member of the masses by this overeducated, patrician fop of a villain.

Why do I hate this man? This sophisticated professional is the answer to Hugh Hefner's rhetorical question: "What kind of a man reads *Playboy?*" Why do I feel a special satisfaction when Columbo hauls him off to jail—humiliated, defeated, professionally destroyed? The answer does not prove difficult: this stuck-up snob of a person thinks his stature and riches make him better than me. So I am happy to learn that he is an insecure egomaniac who maintains his high-salaried "place" only through corruption, and ultimately by murder. What may be a more intriguing question is this: If I already know "who dunnit" and why, and if I know beforehand exactly to what conclusion the episode is leading, why am I sitting here focusing all this attention on the television set?

The second time I watched *Bonanza* I said to my parents (who had recommended the show), "The same things happened this week as last week." They protested, of course. But this is exactly the point: that is why they never missed *Bonanza,* and why I never miss *Columbo,* or *Baretta,* or *Kojak,* or *Harry O,* or, if I can manage to stay home on Saturday night, *The Mary Tyler Moore Show* and *Bob Newhart.* That is why women hospital patients complain that their own doctors are mere shadows compared to Marcus Welby. That is why some Americans haven't missed *The Days of Our Lives* in fifteen years. We don't "just watch TV," we worship there—same time, same station, week after week, at the altar of our own cultural values.

THE "RELIGIOUS" FUNCTIONS OF TELEVISION

William Kuhns, in his excellent study *The Electronic Gospel,* distinguishes several "religious" functions of television.[47] What he points to in television we have been attempting to argue for popular culture generally. Popular culture functions dramatically to reaffirm and support shared societal values and beliefs about life's meaning, from ascertaining the problem to posing the solution. Our continued, regular attendance upon various elements of popular culture (certain TV programs, popular books, the films of certain movie stars, the records of certain country singers, for example) is ritual confirmation that these particular dramas and events effectively embody for us what we value and believe in as Americans. Television is an essentially dramatic medium, with the added advantage that its presentations are regularly scheduled same time, same station—just like church services. Three of Kuhns's ideas will help us here.

1. Originally religion functioned to keep human beings safe and secure from a hostile environment. Religion portrayed the natural forces that threatened human life as the wrath of God or the work of evil spirits and then offered ritual protection from them. Today human life is more and more insulated and extended. Basic needs for food and shelter are not so much in jeopardy as is individual identity. Kuhns writes:

The tall glass-fronted canyons of Manhattan or the four-acre automobile plant tend to reduce the individual to a single function in a gargantual process.[48]

We preach freedom, power, and individualism in America, but everyday life is a living contradiction of this. We move on crowded streets or in suffocating transit systems from our office cubbyhole or place on the assembly line to our wood-frame box house in a suburban development of wood-frame box houses. Television not only reaffirms the beliefs we preach while we are at home, relaxing with a cooling drink, but it also helps to break down the tensions created in us by the looming presence of the impersonal technological environment. The city, whose chaos and confusion overwhelm us, and where we are afraid of other human beings, is ritualistically conquered every week when Kojak or the Rookies identify the problem as a rampant mugger and proceed to reestablish order.

2. Television contains and safeguards "morality, belief, and ritual." Religious myth performs this function by the absolute commitment of the believer to the truth and validity of the myth. In the popular media, TV especially, though this is also true of film, does the same thing in the opposite fashion. The audience is absolutely sure that the characters are *not* real, and that the event never did happen. This assumption shifts the action from everyday life to the level of mythical stereotypes. We can accept, and affirm without a thought of self-contradiction or First Amendment rights, lectures in human ethics back to back with the violent, merciless destruction of vicious criminals—when Kojak delivers both. We know he stand for the world we want to see. The "criminal" he shoots down without hesitation is only a "symbol" of evil, and does not have family, friends, or any redeeming human qualities that might make us feel his loss.

3. Ritual is the dramatization of the victory of order over chaos, of structure over anarchy, of creation over nothingness; and thus of life over death and of good over evil. Television provides this by formula (in dramatic and comedy shows), by format (in quiz, musical, and interview shows), by the policy of reruns, and by

the priority of character pattern over plot developments in its dramatic shows. Marcus Welby and other TV doctors deal not so much with illness or death as with their effect on the meaning of human life. The longest-running and most popular shows have definitely chiseled characters whom we know and love, who represent values in human life in these United States (and in general) that we believe in and can affirm. We tune in not to see what is going to happen, though we are curious about this, but to see how this same character will react to these new circumstances. That the reactions we want to see are the reactions we get is what watching television is all about.

THE TELEVISION FAMILY IN THE BELIEF-SYSTEM MODEL

Television shows come and go. Some types of programs attract viewers in one decade, other types enjoy popularity in another. How do we analyze a belief system when the programs we discuss may be replaced in January? Rather than analyze specific programs individually, and worry about whether anyone will remember them by the time they read our analysis, we will review shows under a thematic category—the family. In this way, since the explication of specific programs serves only to demonstrate the main thesis, the withdrawal of particular shows will in no way render the theme itself irrelevant. "The family" as a category for analysis is limited, however, to its function within the belief-system model. So let's look first at these limitations.

In the dominant American belief system, community

has an important place and "family" might be considered a subgroup in the community.[49] The question concerning the *source* of the evil plaguing the community is *never* answered with reference to a community. The main villain may have henchmen, or a gang, but their internal relationships are the antithesis of what community means in the American value system.[50]

The people who are suffering are always a community in the dominant American belief system. We have called them the "townspeople," and described them as types in Chapter 2. The problem is a break in the interpersonal relations that constitute the community; that is, the problem affects the community as community (in the Western form, the very future of the community itself).

Since the problem is communal, so must be the solution. The classic American belief system asserts that fulfillment equals some situation of permanently restored interpersonal relations. The Western form defines civilization *as* community. All the positive elements of the full human life are found in it—schools, churches, families. The Western is significantly full of family rituals such as marriages and funerals. All good-girl women are family women, and all unmarried men are uncivilized and therefore potentially dangerous. So says the Western form.

Rarely, however, does community effort apply its own deliverance. The deliverer-hero of the dominant American belief system is almost always an individual, as we said (see Chapter 2). The source of the grace shared in the restored community, the power by which the villain is violently defeated—these the deliverer-hero provides. Occasionally a team has delivered us

(The Magnificent Seven, Mission Impossible), but traditionally Americans are suspicious of organization, and do not believe it can rival the effectiveness of the individual. Thus, we have always been delivered by individuals.

The situation may be changing. The effectiveness of the individual diminishes daily, as civilization becomes more complex and as individual identity comes to count for less and less. We are known today by our memberships, and our wallets are full of their cards. If you are a member, you're O.K.—just *try* to rent a car without a major credit card. In our study of the belief-system function of the family in television we will find evidence that reflects this changing situation. Before we turn to that study, we need to clarify a crucial distinction between organizations and communities. All communities are organizations, but all organizations are not communities. A family as the smallest form of community is, therefore, an organization, but all organizations are not families.

The Western form bases its larger community upon the smallest form of community, that is, the family. This has not been lost on modern American corporations. "Ma Bell" puts out a brochure full of pictures of the Bell Telephone "family": males, females, black, white (at least one of each kind). General Motors may refer to its "family." And George Allen's Washington Redskins may call themselves one big "family," praying together in the locker room before and after the games ("the family that prays together, stays together"). Such groups are organizations, but not families. Though they all work together, they are individually members of the organization by reason of special ability, or because of a specialized task they perform for the benefit of the whole. They don't *care* for one another, essentially; they relate to the purpose of the larger organization. Some individual members may be friends and express care and concern for one another. But membership in the organization is not determined by that care, but rather by their ability to serve the larger organization. Authority rests with those who hold the purse strings, and occasionally with those who are greatly accomplished in special skills.

A true family, on the other hand, is constituted by the care of its members for one another, by their loyalty to one another. They do not associate for financial reasons, or for status. Any member of the family group is honored and respected solely because of family membership, and not for any particular skill or ability. The family unit has no purpose larger than its own existence. Authority is based on respect and tradition, supported by love, not by wealth or position.

In the following we will distinguish three types of family program: the family situation comedy, the soap opera, the family as deliverer-hero. Situation comedies are about problems of internal maintenance of the already redeemed community (question five). Soap operas are about a struggling community, beset by evils that overwhelm and destroy the family-community—without much hope for redemption. The third type is fairly new, portraying the family-community not only as a redeemed fellowship (question four), but also as the *source* of deliverance (question three).

THE FAMILY IN TELEVISION

Situation Comedies

Situation comedies are by nature family-based, though with some variety in the structure of the "family." Most of these center around a husband-wife team *(All in the Family, Maude, The Jeffersons, Good Times, Bob Newhart, Rhoda)* or around a partial family unit *(Sanford and Son, Phyllis, That's My Mama).* Two of the most popular involve large "families," none of the members of which are related by marriage: *M*A*S*H* and *The Mary Tyler Moore Show.*

All these programs have one thing in common: the problems with which they deal are never a threat to the continuance of the family-community itself. Each family unit is already securely established. Thus, episodes in situation comedies are never about the survival of community, per se. Rather they assume the unity of a small group of caring people (family) as a natural fact of life. The problems they encounter concern internal adjustments in the family, the everyday coping with which all families must struggle. The programs always begin with the family in its normally smooth-functioning, redeemed state. A problem arises, often a conflict between members of the family or a personal-life problem of one of the members which short-circuits ongoing intra-family relationships. The program is *about* how this problem is resolved, and how the family returns to the harmony with which the program opened. The ending is always happy. We expect this, since we know that deliverance from evil is not necessary.

Examining all of these programs in depth is beyond

the scope of our intent. We want to note, however, two new trends within this subgenre. First, several of these sitcoms make a simplistic hero-villain distinction roughly analogous to the Western form. Secondly, two of the shows display a caring among members of the family group that makes unusual demands on the audience, and that infuses the sitcom formula with a special quality of humanness new to television.

The four obvious examples of the first trend are *All in the Family, Maude, The Jeffersons,* and *Sanford and Son.* None of these shows has a "villain," in the traditional sense, but all of them pinpoint the source of the family's trouble. Normally, these shows put the blame for the family's trouble on the shoulders of one person, a stereotype of the kind of people who cause *us* trouble. Archie Bunker is our favorite bigot; Maude is our favorite bleeding-heart liberal. George Jefferson caricatures the nouveau-riche, upwardly mobile, social snob. Conveniently, he is black, so we have a double assurance: first, that they (the coloreds) are just like everybody else when they get a little money; but at the same time, that George Jefferson is obviously not like *us* (whites are more sophisticated). Redd Foxx's Sanford is the cranky older generation, who though out of touch with the "swing" of things today muddle through on those characteristics we admire about our elders. How refreshing —we learn week after week that however full-blown and hot their rhetoric, these are essentially harmless, lovable people we can laugh at and live with. These are the people with whom *we* must cope, who disturb *our* communal serenity, flies in the nectar of our satisfaction. That we can watch them strut in the ritual drama of weekly TV fare, and witness their foolishness exposed, calms and reassures us that their threat is a family one and can be safely and finally controlled there.

Good Times, in which Maude's maid Florida gets her own show, frequently leans on the cocky, obnoxious (but very funny) eighteen-year-old "J.J." in much the same way as we have been describing. But *Good Times* is much more *Father Knows Best* than *All in the Family* or *Maude,* so it is more traditional than these others.

Bob Newhart, Rhoda, and *Phyllis* also focus regularly on the same character. But these MTM Enterprises shows have a lining of pathos rarely present in other situation comedies. Their outlook on life is less optimistic. Their people are more vulnerable—a little of the schlemiel in all of us plagues their every step. This makes us feel for these characters, the way one would never feel for Archie or Maude. We hurt with them, not the traumatic hurts of great tragedy, but the everyday sinking of the heart as plans go awry, when control over our own circumstances is wrenched from our hands. Still, Bob, Rhoda, and Phyllis live only temporarily in the often hilarious situations we see them muddle through. Their stereotypes have little or no transcendence; we do not care enough.

The families of *The Mary Tyler Moore Show* and *M*A*S*H* extend our caring farther. *The Mary Tyler Moore Show* began as straight situation comedy, but the characters began to grow in their roles, transcending the limits of their sitcom stereotypes. Scenes emerged in which the character interplay had nothing whatever to do with the evening's plot line, but served rather to demonstrate changing self-understanding and correspondingly deepened interpersonal relations between the characters. Whole episodes highlighted personal growth, as when Lou Grant (Edward Asner) had to struggle to overcome his fixed ideas about "that kind of woman" in order to accept his own feelings about his new nightclub vocalist girl friend.

Two early episodes of *The Mary Tyler Moore Show* especially illustrate the direction in which the show is moving. Both involved Lou Grant. In the first, Lou becomes separated from his wife, Edie. She leaves him, because after twenty-six years of marriage she needs to know what it is like to be depressed and not to have him to fall back on. On another occasion, Lou is paired by mistake with an eighty-one-year-old woman. At a dance, he meets his ex-wife, Edie, and in embarrassment introduces the old woman as Mary's friend. Then, turning to Mary, he says, "What have I done?" Mary replies, "You were in a tough spot." Lou responds, "Not that tough." And he proceeds to reintroduce the woman as his date and to dance with her. Carol Traynor Williams writes:

Only a company can make that dull virtue, companionship, a value of power and promise at this point in time. The values underlying MTM are all like companionship —superficially unexciting, banal, "old fashioned" (in fact, conservative), and humanistic. They affirm the complexity of every human being; they parade every butt and foil—not just women, not unmarried women, but eighty-year-old *old* women—and insist (no less stubbornly for their subtlety) that we see their dignity. They achieve their aim, I think, because the complex, sometimes apparently contradictory human characteristics MTM portrays are real human characteristics, and the complex values of human dignity and companionship that underlie and shape the series are real human values that we cherish—perhaps wistfully—beyond all militant fads in "values."[51]

One of the early 1975 episodes found Mary with a case of the "blahs." Rhoda and Phyllis had moved on to new horizons. Mary felt her life was stagnating. The whole newsroom staff rallied to cheer her up. When finally she "resolved" the problem by moving into a new apartment, the cast surprised her with an "apartment warming" for which Ted forgot the wine. As the program ended, the camera panned back from the whole staff sitting in a circle on the floor of Mary's empty apartment, talking quietly, laughing, drinking the newly purchased wine. Lou, Murray, Ted, Sue Ann, Georgette, and Mary—the *Mary Tyler Moore* family at the First Supper.

*M*A*S*H* had worked itself into the hearts of Americans—the ratings proved this. But how strongly the American public was attached to the members of this family became fully apparent only when Colonel Henry Blake was killed in a plane crash. Everyone knew it was his last show; everyone knew that McLean Stevenson was leaving the cast of *M*A*S*H* for his own variety show. The script said only that Henry had been recalled to the States, and that he was leaving to rejoin his wife and family there. Was this not a suitable ending? If the *M*A*S*H* troop is a typical, front-line medical group in a real war, returning home to one's wife and family is dandy. But the *M*A*S*H* characters are a family for us, a small community of human caring, of human kindness, sympathy, understanding, and sacrifice. For Henry to leave this community that we all love, that we wish were our own, is not salvation, it is a fall from grace. Apparently the scriptwriters had sensed this, and they had not even told the cast of the last line of the episode, delivered by Radar in the operating tent. Henry's plane had crashed; there were no survivors. This hurt. Of course, the *M*A*S*H* family is a ritual one. So the closing credits passed over shots of Henry in our happy memories of him, clowning and full of life. An instant resurrection. And, of course, he was back in the reruns the very next week.

Suffering Through the Soap Opera [52]

On any given weekday afternoon, between twelve noon and about four P.M., twenty to thirty million Americans will be watching the longest-running, continually popular form of television programming—the soap opera. Generally, twelve to fourteen different series are available, offering varying plot or character or thematic directions: for example, twenty-three years of character development *(Search for Tomorrow);* life among the medical professionals *(General Hospital, The Doctors, The Guiding Light);* strong central family figures *(Days of Our Lives, As the World Turns);* social relevance *(All My Children, The Young and the Restless, One Life to Live);* strikingly drawn female villains *(Another World, As the World Turns).* To point out the differences between particular soap operas is as essential to understanding the soap opera as to note the differences between snowflakes in describing a snowfall. Every snowflake is unique, and soap opera fans surely feel this way about their favorite programs. Critical analysts argue that some operas are more "realistic" than others, meaning that they "employ more controversial plot twists." Race, women's liberation, abortion, and child abuse are controversial; incest, murder, deceit, adultery, traumatizing guilt, and illegitimate pregnancy are not. Such distinctions miss the point entirely, and, furthermore, are basically erroneous. The soap opera is a rigidly structured, ritual enactment of elements of what many Americans believe and value about life, arranged to present a consistently comprehensive belief system.

Following our belief-system models, our analysis of the soap opera will answer these questions: Who are the people who have the problems addressed by the soap opera? What are the problems? What are the sources of the problems? Is there redemption from these problems, and if so, what is the redeemed situation like? The soap opera offers little hope of redemption. More like the detective story than the Western, the soap opera world view allows only personal fulfillment, and that only temporarily. The soap opera answers the first three questions more than the fourth. So, let us begin with at least an indication of what the fulfilled life would look like, before we turn to the problems and their sources and find that the fulfilled life is ultimately unattainable.

Fulfillment

In the soap opera world view, fulfillment is a happy family life. Many of the major characters are related, either naturally or by marriage. The "bridge over troubled waters" of the soap opera is always a family, anchored in father and mother figures whose role is to suffer with and comfort the rest of the cast. They are good-goods: the Hortons of *Days of Our Lives* are the best-known example, though included might be the

Matthewses of *Another World,* the Hugheses and Stewarts of *As the World Turns,* and the Tylers of *All My Children.* When illness, divorce, incest, or murder happens to a family member or is committed by one, Father Horton provides rational control and long-term strategies, and becomes the family spokesman. Mother Horton is the family crying towel and security blanket. She is intellectually her husband's inferior, as he is inferior to her emotionally and spiritually. Together they hold the family together.

The most glaring example of the redemptive quality of a happy family life is the transformation (however temporary) of the character of Rachel in *Another World.* Marriage to a wealthy older man—but a marriage based on love rather than money—has changed Rachel from one of the most famous "evil woman" villains in soap-opera history into an affectionate, loving person, capable of helping other people.

The Cast

In the Western form, the people who have the problem are the "townspeople." They represent the ongoing social institutions we respect, and they embody the human vulnerability that makes them basically unable to defeat the villain. The women are both the stable center of civilization and more vulnerable to the villain's evil intentions than are the men. The townsmen are physically aggressive and brave (though still nowhere near strong enough to counter the villain), though normally adolescent and irresponsible prior to domestication (marriage). The soap opera continues these conventions.

The cast of the soap opera is significantly uniform.

The characters are white, Anglo-Saxon, and middle-class, with very few exceptions. They also tend to be high-status professionals. They conveniently mix what is with what ought to be. They are what we are (Middle Americans), *and* what we would like to be (high-status professionals). Their professional status makes eaves-dropping on their private lives interesting for us. We all know that people who earn a lot of money don't have to work very hard at what they do, and we are used to having our heroes and heroines standing around with time on their hands. Here the money they earn makes their casual, leisure-time style credible.

Soap operas feature heroines almost exclusively. Only occasionally do men become the center of the plots. Still, the total cast of characters is usually distributed equally between males and females. At one point *The Guiding Light* and *The Edge of Night* each had seven males and seven females in its cast: of the fourteen males, five were medical doctors, three were lawyers, two ran a nightclub, one was in big business, one a newspaper reporter, one a psychiatrist, and one drove a taxi, though he was the son of a doctor. Of the females, one was a doctor, one a lawyer, one a fashion designer, one a part-time nightclub entertainer, five were secre-taries, and five were housewives. The role conventions of the sexes in the soap opera call for each to have a dual character. The men are basically brave, handsome, in-telligent, quite desirable and generally marvelous hu-man beings. But they have a fatal flaw—though they seem sensational persons, and may be fine at their jobs and in appearance, they are actually incredibly naïve and possess absolutely no ability to resist temptation, particularly sexual temptation. The soap-opera women,

on the other hand, are strong—they both create and
solve most of the problems. While men are ineffectual,
the least bit of loving intervention by a female is redemptive. But the women have a flaw as well—they are
passive and subservient in any situation in which a man
is involved. Anthony Astrachan writes:

The women are strangely submissive to the men when
it comes to the fundamental questions of society, like a
married woman's working. On "As the World Turns,"
no woman who is living happily with her husband has
a job. On "Another World," Lenore Delaney gave up
her job when her husband said she had to choose between the job and him.[53]

The Problem

The soap opera fascinates its viewer by unraveling
the plot-line development consistently in a setting that
establishes its point visually. Here, truly, the medium is
the message. Soap operas accomplish this by a clever
interface of what we see and what we hear. In the midst
of this interface we find the problem of the soap-opera
view of life and its various sources.

The symbols of being a successful (professional) middle-class American are integral to the sets: book-lined
library shelves and silver tea services (though soap-
opera people drink mostly coffee). The sets themselves
are apartments, offices, or hospital nooks and crannies
—claustrophobic space; we are locked in with our
doubts, fears, and emotions. What we must face here
are close, personal, life-shattering issues, not general
social problems. Where we live every day, with family,
with relatives, where we rub up against other individual human beings, the soap opera takes place. The rest

of the world is locked out, as we are locked in. We cannot escape into anonymity, into the objective world of casual noninvolvement with persons. The soap-opera set itself enforces this psychological mood. So does the action. Ninety-nine percent of soap-opera action is dialogue—over coffee, on the phone, in subdued living-room conversational tone, except of course the passionate outbursts.

The ironic interface of what we see (the sets, characters) with what we hear being discussed is of the essence in the soap opera. What we see is standard fare. They never go white-water rafting or mountain-climbing or to football games or to the movies. They do all the time what we do most of the time. But while they sip coffee or talk on the phone they are discussing issues of life, death, tragedy, chaos, and sorrow. The amount of humor in the soap opera is so infinitesimally small as to be negligible. The problem of the soap opera is not how to share or spread or more fully enjoy some form of happiness. The problem of the soap opera is the overwhelmed life, the life in which interpersonal relations have been shattered or brought to the brink of disruptive chaos and confusion.

Soap-opera characters suffer from the breakup of happy family situations. They suffer jealousy, guilt, alcoholism, various sorts of mental and physical diseases, insecurity, infidelity, adolescent trauma, sterility, pregnancy, betrayal, and so on. But they are never ambiguously the source of their own problems. And so what they suffer is often destructive of meaning because it is incomprehensible, or because it seems tragically unfair or unjust. The despairing pessimism and hopelessness that results contributes to the fascination by which the soap opera holds its viewers.

Superficially the men and women of the soap opera cause each others' problems. Evil women victimize the men. The sexual temptation that men cannot seem to resist ultimately reduces them to victims. While we sit in the audience and go up the walls of our living rooms in frustration, evil women repeatedly turn gullible men away from their wives and sweethearts. Any soap-opera woman, whether evil or not, can cause a soap-opera man's blood to pump furiously at the slightest turn of attention in his direction.

The victimization of men by women pales before the willingness of women repeatedly to suffer at the hands of men. In *As the World Turns,* Kim Dixon, who married Dr. John Dixon only to give her baby (fathered by her brother-in-law) a name, tried to leave him after she finally lost the baby. He not only blackmailed her into staying, but after she was reconciled with her sister and had decided finally to leave him he prolonged the effects of an injury that hospitalized him in order to bind her to him. In *The Guiding Light,* Ken, undiagnosed paranoid psychotic, badgered his loyal and loving wife Janet into leaving him with continued, totally unfounded, accusations about her infidelity. But she loves him, and so they keep having reconciliations, the result of which is *always* that she gets hurt again. But she keeps coming back for more. Victimization, however, is more a *part* of the problem than a source.

The Source of the Problem

Soap operas support the belief that teeming and seething in chaotic turmoil beneath the order and boring routines of everyday life, waiting to break through the routine and to destroy life, are three main sources of all our problems: (1) the deserved tragedy of just retribution for engaging in illicit sex; (2) the undeserved, life-destroying tragedy of overwhelming, uncontrollable circumstances; and (3) the unredeemably evil person, usually a woman, always the incarnation of evil itself.

Though sterility is a problem in the soap opera, pregnancy is a freighted problem: "All women and girls who engage in premarital or extramarital sex, through seduction, stupidity, or rape, will end up pregnant." As in the romance magazines, such sinfulness—the allowing of the potential chaos of sex to surface—always must be paid for: "Retribution will strike down the most secretive and recalcitrant of sinners."[54] It matters not who was at fault, illicit sex brings dire retribution on the participants. Ripples of implication swell to an unholy roar, shaking the foundations of the most solidly established happy life. The message is loud and clear to the housewives of America: you had better stick to the vicarious experience we provide, and keep your own house in order. We can feel simultaneously wicked and self-righteous—unless, of course, we have transgressed in our own experience. But then we probably wouldn't be sitting home watching the soap opera.

Illness and disease represent the undeserved tragedy of overwhelming circumstances in the soap opera. These certainly come upon us unaware. Soap-opera characters seldom have cancer or hysterectomies. They have syringomyelia or Ubanda fever. It hardly matters that one is actually a disease and the other a fiction—they sound equally alien and uncontrollable, equally mysterious and exotic.

The third source of evil is the purely evil person. These people are particularly vicious and unmerciful, and they are usually women (as Erica Kane in *All My Children,* Lisa Shea in *As the World Turns,* Rachel Frame and Liz Matthews in *Another World*). Here the Eve-as-the-Temptress theme continues still inherent in the culture, and surfacing also in country music and romance magazines. So convincing are these evil women that stories of assault on those who play them by irate fans (as happened to Eileen Fulton, who plays Lisa Shea) are not uncommon.

The setting and mood of the soap opera is a despair from which there is virtually no relief. Yet the main characters endure. They cope, even in a world of suffocating, seemingly unending personal catastrophes. In their perseverance, we are reassured. Still, we cherish other dreams, of more successful communal fulfillment, a life with others that heals and fills our human yearning to satisfaction. Hence, the popularity of *The Waltons.*

The Family as Deliverer-Hero

The family as the community of fulfillment is familiar to us. But in the Western form only individuals deliver us to that community life. The notion that the community of fulfillment might also *provide* the very fulfillment it institutionalizes is new. Yet expressions of this possibility have arisen in television in recent years. Lone deliverer-heroes have given way to teams, who through concerted cooperation deliver the community from evil. *Ironsides, Police Woman, The Rookies, Police Story,* and even *Kojak* are examples of this trend.

Perhaps the clearest example of the community of

fulfillment functioning as deliverer-hero is *The Waltons*. Three generations, representing the past, the present, and the future in human life, live together in an ideal human community. Set in the depression era, and in the country, *The Waltons* uses nostalgia to idealize its human family. From our perspective of an urban culture beset with social issues of cosmic dimensions, nostalgia for the simple life in the country has a powerful appeal. Moreover, a time of external crisis forces us all to work together as brothers and sisters against the common enemy (as we did in World War II).

The Walton family centers around the father, John Walton, and the mother, Olivia. Anne Roiphe writes of the father:

John Walton, as played by actor Ralph Waite, is a strong, honest, gentle, kind, stubborn, self-contained, uncompromised man, a man who takes responsibility, who is patient, understanding, devoted, open, without prejudice or fear—the kind of father that would make growing up seem part of an orderly natural process, not the intricate, crippling, weaseling around it seems to be for most people . . . who carries his sick child in his arms to the hospital, who teaches an arrogant young Baptist preacher humility and grace, who protects a troubled juvenile delinquent, who teaches trust and honor, love for all God's creatures to his children.[55]

Olivia Walton is a woman of deep-down beauty of soul, of the earth itself; love shines in her eyes, pouring forth in compassionate concern for her children. When she is bedridden with polio and her own personal determination does not seem sufficient to conquer the dread disease, one of her children cries out in the night. With a strength far beyond her simple, individual capacity, she overcomes the illness and goes immediately to meet the child's need. She does not merely give of agape—the totally devoted, self-sacrificing love of the New Testament—she is that love incarnate. Anne Roiphe writes of Olivia Walton:

She washes, cooks, cleans, irons, shops, gardens, sews, tends the animals, helps with homework, goes to church —all without the aid of modern-day appliances. She mothers all children, drifters and outcasts who for plot reasons find their way to Walton's Mountain. . . . She works hard and does not despise herself or her occupation, and her emotional importance to all around her is so clear that it is no wonder she walks with such pride and her smile is so deep. She is the mother we all wish we had. She is the mother we all would like to be. She is the image that gives us guilt on days when we are irritable or tired, when we are selfish, when we wander away from home, when we fail to stay married; when we produce children who drop out of school, turn to drugs; when we can't find what's wrong or remember how to talk to our parents or how to explain to ourselves the disappointments that line the edges of our lives.[56]

The formula of the program requires that tensions arise between the members of the family (pick any two) either as a result of the appearance on Walton's Mountain of visitors from the outside world, or as a result of conflict between the mutual giving or growth of the family community and the assertive development of some family member's individual life. In the former case, the intra-family tension may be a subplot, with the major attention directed to the metaphorical "sickness" of the visitor, which may be suspiciousness, pretentiousness, humorlessness, a fear of needing other people.

The resolution of the story reveals that the Walton family is not only the *place* of fulfillment, that is, the perfect interpersonal community of love and understanding, but is, as well, the *source* of the grace by which life is made whole. The family heals the broken life of the visitor. Here *The Waltons* reverses the tradition of the classic American belief system in which an individual deliverer restores unity and future wholeness to the fractured or besieged community. In this case healing comes through contact with the redeemed community.

When the plot describes the conflict of an individual member's life plans with the growth of the family-community, the tension is always resolved in favor of the family-community. The individual member comes to see the selfishness or thoughtlessness of his/her personal ambitions, or to realize that a slight alteration of plans will bring them in line with the family's future, to everyone's mutual advantage. Clearly, the fulfillment of the individual *within* the communal structure is superior to an individual fulfillment that sets the person against or outside of the growth of the community. This is classically American, and illustrates the preference in American cultural life for the values of the dominant belief system over the subdominant set of values concerning individual fulfillment. Even in popular magazines, which are the "scriptures" of the subdominant belief system, individual fulfillment is often essentially communal, as in *Ladies' Home Journal, Ms.,* and sometimes in men's outdoor-adventure magazines. In the Walton plot formula, the family-community is the *source* of effective fulfillment for the individual, who grows into a more complete human individual through the love and understanding of the family.

As in the value system of country music, part of the "magic" of the Walton healing power is derived from the rural setting. It's good to be a community member. If your community is a country one, that's even better. The "country setting" of *The Waltons* is similar to that of Dolly Parton's "Tennessee Mountain Home"; it is more anti-city than anything else.

The mind-draining work of the farm laborer, the bone-wearying, imagination-crushing work of the farmer and his wife are always forgotten as we think of wonderful things like homemade jellies and herb gardens and zinnias and sunflowers growing full in dark soil.[57]

Where the city stinks, the country smells fresh and sweet. The city has crammed schedules and crowded days, the country has the slow pace of the natural rhythm of life, allowing time for conversation. Where the city is "stop and go," laws and regulations, waiting in line, and moving with the crowd, the country is free-roaming in dusty fields and cool woodlands. The city is an earsplitting din; the country is, above all, quiet. *The Waltons* episodes end with a dramatization of this: as the camera pulls back into the pitch-black night, lighted only by the bedroom lights of the Walton house, we can hear—from what must be a hundred yards away—the members of the family saying good night to each other. "Good night, Ma." "Goodnight, Pa." "Goodnight, John-Boy."

Surely nothing we know can rival such peace.

7

Detective Fiction: DECLINING HOPE FOR THE FUTURE

From Sir Arthur Conan Doyle to this century's Agatha Christie and Erle Stanley Gardner, traditional detective fiction has concentrated on solving the crime by logically deducing the criminal from the clues. It was more *detecting* fiction than detective fiction. The rational process of discovering who did it, and how, completely overshadowed the person of the detective, though the best known of the detectors (e.g., Holmes, Poirot, Miss Marple, Perry Mason, Nero Wolfe) certainly have personality. The classic detective is more intellect than emotion, so much more that we would be shocked if anger ever became a major motivation in his activities. "Hard-boiled" detective fiction, on the other hand, as introduced by Raymond Chandler and Dashiell Hammett, is as much about the detective as about the particular crime or its solution. An intellect is still at work, but in a body frustrated by guilt, physical mistreatment, moral ambiguities, overindulgence, and growing old. The intelligence guiding the operation makes mistakes by overvaluing its own analysis and underestimating the perversity of its foe. Understandably, tenacity and luck prevail in the detective story, just as logic ultimately reigned in the classic detective tale.

Fundamental to the classic detecting story is the assumption that the world is ordered and rational. For everything there is a reason, for every effect a cause. A crime is an unexplained event, temporarily breaking the smooth operation of the social contract. The classic detector, by figuring out and describing for us the events constituting the crime, sets these events in their proper order and restores divinely intended tranquillity to the community.

The world of the modern detective is more familiar to us: it is the modern America in which we live. Tranquillity, peace, and order are seldom found. Rather, corruption, cheating, duplicity, violence, and perversion abound. All that glitters in this world is false facade, built on suspicion and greed. No one can be trusted—all social roles are poses, shifting like shadows, stretching reality to fit the focused light. The end tables of this world are dusty, the rugs are dirty, and the lighted neon signs have a letter burned out. It is the world of prostitution and dope, of sleazy motels and greasy chili. In this world money is more important than life. The poor live in despair and jealousy while the rich mask their decadent souls in wild and arrogant material consumption.

The symbolic focus of this world in the modern detective novel is, of course, the city. Our world is not merely social or communal, it is urban. No one city is particularly singled out, for the "city" of the detective novel is the "city" of our fearing yet fascinated imagination. However corrupt and terrifying this "city" may be, the lure of its strange thrills and whispered satisfactions and its intriguing promise of power hold us in rapt attention. Here is the city not commonly known as "inner city," but the city of downtown and suburbs and exurbia combined—the "city" we carry around in our heads. To those who conquer and rule it, this "city" promises wealth, position, power. To the rest of us it offers material goods and anonymity to mask the means of their acquisition. In short, everybody cheats on his income tax, but nobody talks about it.

The American fascination with the "gangster," wrote Robert Warshow in the early 1950's, is evidence that American self-understanding has been coming under the domination of this "city" for several decades.[58] The significance of the gangster in American popular culture does not reflect the significance of the gangster in American life, Warshow notes, since "most Americans have never seen a gangster." Yet we identify with the movie and television "gangster" because he is "the man of the city," the skilled survivor who knows the city, who beats it, who comes to own it. The gangster personifies the "city" of our imagination; "he is what we want to be and what we are afraid to become." Vicariously we release our frustrations through his dominance and control, through his violence, through his sadistic revenge. The aim of the gangster, Warshow continues, is to control everyone else for his own personal pleasure and satisfaction—to become the absolutely invulnerable individual. One must emerge from and dominate the crowd, or one is nothing. Every gangster expresses our lust to "be somebody." So, in the popular media, the gangster must always rise steadily to wealth and success in order for us to identify with his victories. Then he must quickly and decisively fall in order for our fears to be quieted and our moral vision to be sustained. This, Warshow concludes, is the tragic irony of the gangster, the pessimism with which the "city" of our imagination cloaks our belief in the individual: "It is dangerous to be alone." We immediately understand when we see a gangster alone that he is about to be killed. "And yet the very conditions of success make it impossible not to be alone, for success is always the establishment of an individual preeminence that must be imposed on others, in whom it automatically arouses hatred." Thus, the drive that establishes and sustains the gangster, and by which we are so attracted and awed, is at the same time the cause of his demise.

So it is with the detective. Like the gangster he is the skilled survivor. But our identification with the detective is more complete. It divests itself of the ambivalence of the attraction-fear relationship we have with the gangster. The detective rises above the turmoil and red tape of the city's institutions and succeeds where others fail. He is a hero and a deliverer because his "success" is not wealth or power, but justice and righteousness. And he does not fail. His victory may not be clean, clear, and simple (it may leave scars and a bad taste in the mouth), but it is satisfying to us, as is the morality reaffirmed in the final demise of the gangster.

This detective is not a "real life" person. He is the detective as deliverer in the city of our imaginative self-understanding. We know this man: he was played by Humphrey Bogart in *The Maltese Falcon* and *The Big Sleep*. In his well-known essay, Raymond Chandler describes this deliverer (notice how well it fits our image of Bogart):

Down these mean streets a man must go who is not himself mean, who is neither tarnished nor afraid. . . . He must be the best man in his world and a good enough man for any world. . . . If there were enough like him, the world would be a safe place to live in, without becoming too dull to be worth living in.[59]

Obviously, the modern detective story urbanizes the Western, creating a new form by placing the Western drama in an anti-Western context (see Chapters 2 and 3). The Western drama—which involved the appearance of evil as a threat to the future welfare of the community, the incarnation of good in a deliverer-champion, the justified violence by which this deliverer destroys the evil force, and the restorative hope prompted by the victory of righteousness—is continued in the detective novel. However, the eschatological elements are compromised. Good and evil are still simplistically differentiated in the detective novel, but the embodiment of good is a stained and tarnished one, and the violent confrontation of the hero and the villain is not the *final* confrontation, it is only one of a series. The townspeople are no longer clearly innocent and the villains now live in the community itself. It becomes much more difficult to tell the "good guys" from the "bad guys." Everybody is guilty of something, but the villain is guilty of a lot more than most of us. The defeat of this villain does not mean the final victory of civilization over alien anarchy. It only signals a temporary reaffirmation of the presence and power of good, and reasserts the belief that justice will ultimately prevail. The victory of the hero does not bring the final purification; we retain much of the guilt and anxious frustration inevitably characteristic of this life. As Chandler said, "It is not a fragrant world, but it is the world you live in."

The action of the detective novel is Western, but the mood is anti-Western. One of the first anti-Western films, *Bad Day at Black Rock,* combines the Western setting with the solution of a crime and the deliverance of the criminals—all respected community citizens—to the police. The hero of the detective novel is certainly as honorable and admirable as the classic Western deliverer, but the arena of his activity is a much less perfect society. The woman he defends, far from being chaste, may already have been debauched by the villain before the hero meets her. The rich men and women who hire the detective are themselves despised by him, for their unfounded arrogance rather than for their wealth or position. As Chandler said, "Philip Marlowe and I do not despise the upper classes because they take baths and have money; we despise them because they are phoney."[60] No longer are the good people the ones who live in the community while the evil villains are those who live outside. Good people and evil people are distinguishable; only the standards of categorizing are more ambiguous. At least they are not equitable with community membership or social position. In any case, the reader is meant to identify with the detective and the good people; so the "externality of evil" principle we pointed to in the Western form still applies in the detective novel.

The transition of the hero-deliverer figure from the fantasy superhero, to the classic Western deliverer, to the urbanized detective might be described in this way. Recall what we said of this hero above (Chapters 1 and 2), especially that he combines qualities of essential humanity (so that we can identify with him) and qualities of superhuman skill and cunning (so that he may believably deliver us where we know we cannot deliver ourselves). In the fantasy hero, the uncommon, superhuman qualities far outweigh the human, common ones. Comic fantasy heroes like the Lone Ranger, the pulp-fiction superheroes like James Bond, have little if any really human qualities. They have no doubts, they make few mistakes, they are hardly cynical. In the Western drama, the human qualities fairly balance the superhuman. Western heroes often have community counterparts (inheritors of the torch) who demonstrate to us what the humanity of the hero would look like in a civilized, established community model. The detective novel raises the human qualities above the superhuman —the detective is human, and above all fallible. He delivers us more through luck, stubborn perseverance, and honed natural (and physical) instincts than through superpower, superweapons, or kung-fu fighting ability.

Popular literature is the detective's home territory. Today's successors of Marlowe are Ross Macdonald's Lew Archer (named for Sam Spade's partner in *The Maltese Falcon*) and John D. MacDonald's Travis McGee. Ross Macdonald is the better weaver of plot and an unequaled unraveler of the skein of human interpersonal relations. He has inherited Chandler's locale as well: the tawdry, slick, sleazy neon world of Southern California. But Lew Archer is more a mirror than a person in his own right; an efficient deliverer, but one with whom we can barely and rarely identify. In our terminology, Archer serves the dominant myth, but not the subdominant one. Adequate to both is John D. MacDonald's Travis McGee.

TRAVIS MCGEE, TARNISHED KNIGHT IN MODERN ARMOR

When *The Dreadful Lemon Sky,* MacDonald's six-
teenth in the Travis McGee series, received wide critical attention, the public discovered a character that had
been developed long before. The series is not progressive. Travis McGee is as quintessentially present in *The
Deep Blue Good-by,* number one in the series which
began in 1964, as he is in 1975's much-acclaimed
Lemon Sky. A system of beliefs consistent in its values
operates throughout the sixteen books. The self-affirma-
tion of the classic Western belief system merges with
the self-hatred, guilt, and bitterness of the anti-Western. Romantic, individualist hero Travis McGee man-
ages again and again to save some of the good ones from
some of the bad ones, and to destroy the latter in the
process. The formula is simple, but the context is complex. Before we examine that context, something must
be said about the cast of characters called the "townspeople."

The townspeople, according to our analysis of the
Western form (Chapter 2), are those endangered by the
villain. As noted above, four types of people dominate
the town: women, inheritors-of-the-torch figures, supports and sidekicks, and corrupt bureaucrats. McGee's
world continues to involve this traditional set, though in
slightly altered arrangement. Villainous, corrupt
bureaucrats abound, as we shall see. Since in the detective genre the community as a whole can never be fully
redeemed, the inheritor-of-the-torch figure of the
Western drama has no direct parallel. MacDonald gives
McGee a combination of sidekick and inheritor of the

torch in Meyer, a retired economist-philosopher, who complements McGee's natural instincts with rationality. Meyer accompanies and assists McGee as sidekicks traditionally do, while representing in his sensitivity and insights some of the best characteristics of the human animal, normally a function of the inheritor of the torch. Other supporter persons—such as lawyers and professional photographers—appear from time to time throughout the series.

MacDonald continues in the McGee series the dual role of women as they appear among the Western's townspeople. The Western's good girl—normally a schoolmarm or rancher's daughter cut to the virginal, future wife/mother mold—appears as companion-assistant to McGee. But MacDonald defines her "goodness" somewhat differently. As the source of sexual, romantic involvement for McGee, she is "good" because of her open, healthy attitude toward sex. She treasures the sharing of the act; she would never use this relationship as a means to some other end. McGee likes women tall and muscular, with the physical conditioning of professional dancers. Twenty women in the sixteen books fit this description. McGee pursues the villain aided by Meyer and this female companion, who in the chase barely escape defilement, injury, or death. Meyer is almost killed in three novels in a row, two women *are* killed, one dies of cancer, one gets her head smashed in but lives.

MacDonald's alteration of the Western's other woman, the woman of dubious virtue, parallels his description of the good girl. The Western form presents the bad girl as antithetical to the good-girl heroine. The good girl confines her sexual activities to the family, the bad girl is sexually promiscuous, or worst of all, is *availa-ble* to the villain! Yet the Western holds out the possibil-ity of her redemption. She may be morally corrupt, but her soul is pure. MacDonald's good girl respects sex for the human sharing of the act itself; the bad girl is a cold, calculating, selfish sexual athlete. She uses sex for some-thing other than itself, never joining the sex act with emotional commitment to the partner. Of the nine out-standing examples of this type, two are prostitutes, two are collectors of sexual trophies, one wants to make Travis McGee her concubine, one is just a fun-loving party girl. The other three, though they appear in three different books, are girl Fridays to high-class villains, and all three specialize in sexual satisfaction. Though McGee eventually sleeps with two or three of that type, they cloy and depress his spirit. Generally, he will have none of it, for reasons he never tires of preaching about. In *The Quick Red Fox* he says it best:

Wisdom says the only values are the ones you place on yourself. . . . Though I have faltered from time to time, I do want the relationship, if it does become intimate, to rest solidly on trust, affection, respect. Not just for taking, or scoring, or using, or proving anything. . . . Not for recreation, not for health rationalizations, nor for sociologically constructive contacts. But because she is a woman, and valuable. And you are a man, and equally valuable. . . . Break down, McGee. Say it. Okay, for love and love alone.[61]

McGee the romantic comes through loud and clear. Most of the plots describe McGee's wrathful avenging of a victimized and innocent townsperson. These "born victims," as McGee often calls them, are naïve, disaster-prone people in a world of scavenger wolves. Growing up in a perverse, preying culture, they never had a chance—at least until Travis McGee came along. Let us turn to a detailed analysis of McGee, his world, and his opponents.

What Is Evil?

From what must the victimized townspeople be delivered? In the Western, a deliverer-hero must rescue the townspeople, since they do not have the ability to extricate themselves. The detective story features the same heroic rescue, but the background for these saving exploits in the detective novel is anti-Western. MacDonald sketches a multidimensional world that is unrelentingly anti-Western. In *A Tan and Sandy Silence,* McGee lies in a motel room, trying to digest a "roast beef sandwich which lay in my stomach like a dead armadillo," watching a TV news report:

Droughts and murders. Inflation and balance of payments. Drugs and demonstrations. Body counts and new juntas. . . . News has always been bad. The tiger that lives in the forest just ate your wife and kids, Joe. There are no fat grub worms under the rotten logs this year, Al. Those sickies in the village on the other side of the mountain are training hairy mammoths to stomp us flat, Pete. They nailed up two thieves and one crackpot, Mary. . . . We all become even more convinced that everything has gone rotten, and there is no hope at all, no hope at all. In a world of no hope the motto is *semper fidelis,* which means in translation, "Every week is screw-your-buddy week and his wife too, if he's out of town."[62]

This sounds blatantly negative, despairing, and simplistic. And it is. But MacDonald, though famous for his mini-sermons on specific subjects, rarely indulges in superficial, nihilistic broadsides. To fully appreciate MacDonald's symphonic depiction of the world in which Travis McGee lives and operates (and we ourselves), we need to separate out and examine in detail some of its motifs.

The problem situation itself has four dimensions. The most general and least tractable we will call "the ongoing world situation." MacDonald holds out very little hope for its redemption: it is anti-Western to the core. McGee preaches continuously about its conditions, and occasionally takes precautions against falling victim to it—but he cannot change it, and he seldom tries. Dimensions two and three provide the plot focus. The former is the *societal* imbalance caused by the villain's activities; the latter involves *personal* catastrophe, usually a by-product of the crime that caused the societal imbalance. McGee effectively resolves the problems in both of these dimensions. The fourth dimension pervades the other three, and shares some of the qualities of each. McGee's world is booby-trapped—things are never what they seem. Deception abounds. This quality of the world we will call "hypocrisy," people masquerading as other than what they are. In many ways, hypocrisy is a characteristic of the "ongoing world situation," and can never be fully exposed and eradicated. But as Superman's X-ray vision sees through walls, McGee's gaze penetrates hypocrisy's false front. Hypocrisy may continue, but McGee will shatter the pretense of individual hypocrites. Let us examine and illustrate these dimensions in more detail.

The Ongoing World Situation

In addition to the particular problem situation spawning a particular adventure, McGee's world continually has some anti-Western features that are never really resolved. The most prominent among these he often calls "the structured society." This society is "structured" in two ways. First, to the naked eye, the structured society is row after row of "plastic houses," full of "plastic people," all tending identical flower gardens.[63] Shopping centers mark the center of their social activity. Wire-service newspapers dull the minds of the plastic people with "self-congratulatory pap." The television they watch is amorphous and bland, avoiding offending a few in order to please everybody. Their schools stress adjustment and happiness, while stifling originality and dissent. Their churches are "weekly votes of confidence in God." Their politicians smile and say what everyone wants to hear. The products they spend their hard-earned money to possess are strikingly packaged and fall apart soon.

Underlying what we see is a second kind of structuring. This invisible structure molds the plastic people "to life on the run." Every act is a means toward some still-illusive end. Every movement, every intention, is designed, discussed, organized, planned, processed, incorporated. Even recreation is "scheduled on . . . a tight and competitive basis." Only after having escaped the "senior citizens community" by dying, are these people handed over to the "grief-therapist" whose job it is to "gather them in, rosy their cheeks, close the box and lower them to the only rest they have ever known."

Environmental pollution receives more specific attention than the general target of a "structured society." Manhattan, Chicago, San Francisco, Mexico City, Bradenton, Tampa are all cities McGee cites as monumentally devoted to the worst possible side effects of technological progress. Real estate developers scourge the land, disturbing natural wildlife balance, and rendering ecological disaster. Wells, lakes, island waters, the Everglades—McGee runs into industrial pollution everywhere.

One typical anti-Western feature (see Chapter 3) of the McGee world deserves some attention. The American individual is disappearing, succumbing to group identity, and there is no room for mavericks. Occasionally, McGee gets slightly paranoid about the conspiracy to weed out his kind, the nonconformist individual:

Every once in a while I . . . get the feeling that this is the last time in history when the offbeats like me will have a chance to live free in the nooks and crannies of the huge and rigid structure of an increasingly codified society. Fifty years from now I would be hunted down in the street. They would drill little holes in my skull and make me sensible and reliable and adjusted.[64]

At times, this group pressure takes on another dimension, death itself. McGee calls this side of society's face anonymously "They." When "They" strike down a fellow nonconforming individualist and friend, McGee's burning anger is bent not so much toward revenge as toward the need to affirm life in protest. Walking on the beach alone, he thinks:

The sea and the night sky can make death a small thing. . . . But Sam was still there, in a ghastly dying sprawl on the floor of my mind. . . . They had closed his account. I squatted on my heels and picked up a handful of sand

and clenched it until my shoulder muscles creaked and my wrist ached like an infected tooth. This time they had taken one of mine. One of the displaced ones. A fellow refugee from a plastic structured culture, uninsured, unadjusted, unconvinced. . . . So I had to have a word or two with the account closers. . . . It wasn't dramatics. It wasn't a juvenile taste for vengeance. It was just a cold, searching, speculative curiosity. What makes you people think it's so easy? That was the question I wanted to ask them. I would ask the question even though I already had the answer. It isn't.[65]

It doesn't even have to be a friend, or a nonconforming compatriot. Life in its very essence is a death protest, marked off against and defined by death. As McGee says in *The Dreadful Lemon Sky:* "Death is the genuine definition of reality." So in *A Purple Place for Dying,* when a woman McGee has barely met is suddenly struck down in his presence by a high-powered rifle bullet, McGee cannot leave the case in the hands of admittedly competent police. There is more involved.

Somehow it was identified with my own mortality, my own inevitable day to die. . . . That memorable clunking sound of heavy lead into her vulnerable back, through her pretty silk blouse, had touched something way below my level of consciousness. It roiled something up down there, something fairly nasty, and ancient and invisible.[66]

Death and plastic society are rather amorphous enemies; McGee understandably is more at home with thieves and murderers.

The Societal Balance

Typically the detective novel assumes that something has disturbed society's balance. The detective must restore that balance. For MacDonald, the societal balance is disturbed when the strong exploit the weak. Someone with physical or economic power takes advantage of someone with virtually no ability to fight back. Since organized efforts to correct the injustice are inadequate, which the Western form always assumes, the detective hero steps in to straighten things out.

In Travis McGee's world there are two types of societal imbalance, direct (illegal) and indirect (legal). The former involves theft, murder, or defilement (always of a woman, and always sexual), or some combination thereof. Indirect or legal societal imbalance results from manipulative exploitation, during which strong people use weak people for their own economic, political, and social aggrandizement.

The problem situation will always be one in which someone has been robbed, murdered, or defiled, and may include or involve manipulative exploitation as well.

Personal Catastrophe

As a direct result of the problem of societal imbalance in the Travis McGee novel, personally distraught and ravaged human beings appear, in dire need of the restoration of their individual health and life spirit. In fourteen of the approximately twenty-two such occurrences in the sixteen novels, the suffering person is a sexually attractive female restored to health and happiness by McGee's personal brand of therapy. One is prompted to call this pattern the "wounded-bird syndrome." On five occasions McGee is himself nursed back to health by nubile female friends. Four other restorations are mutually undertaken.

MacDonald claims that somehow individuals get their personal wholeness ground up in the process of restoring the societal balance, and that these individuals need a special kind of therapy. Exactly how they are returned to health and happiness we will see shortly.

Hypocrisy

In *The Dreadful Lemon Sky*, McGee comments, "I am suspicious of anything which tries to look like something it isn't." Everything in McGee's world is tainted with efforts to accomplish exactly that, to look like something or someone it isn't. Defensive and aggressive forms of hypocrisy are everywhere. The former has no intended malice; it is merely part of the way we pretend, often to hide our true feelings, as McGee notices when a tall, stunning blonde's "warm and welcoming" smile does not completely mask a cold distance in her eyes. We may try to dress and act a part merely to impress people with our importance. In *One Fearful Yellow Eye*, McGee describes a sculptor who insists his representation of dogs copulating is high art:

Kirstarian turned very slowly to face us. I was astonished to see how young his face and his eyes were in that small area not obscured by the huge, untrimmed black beard. He wore the kind of black suit favored by European intellectuals, and I had thought from the shape of him that he was at least middle aged. But he was merely a plump young man with bad posture.[67]

Every now and then McGee announces to other characters that he is "impatient with fraud, . . . with all pretentious and phoney people." Or other characters remark how wonderful it is to deal with someone like McGee, someone refreshingly honest and unwilling to play the usual social games, someone who refuses to con an old woman with "sweet lies and gentle talk." There are times, however, when McGee himself purposely dresses or acts in a deceptive way to get information or to fool the villain. He knows that people will make quick evaluative judgments, and he is eager to provide misleading information about himself to that end.

There is, of course, a more directly aggressive hypocrisy. In fact, a terrifyingly intentional duplicity. Mac-Donald is never more effective in communicating the danger of a world constantly pretending it is something other than it is, than when he matches Travis McGee against one of his patented smiling villains. Occasionally, we meet a smiling person we know well, as in *Bright Orange for the Shroud:*

After long minutes the door opened and Calvin Stebber came smiling into the room. . . . He marched up to me and stared up at me, smiling, and I could feel the impact of his superb projection of warmth, interest, kindliness, importance. You could be the man's lifelong friend after ten minutes, and marvel that he found you interesting enough to spend a piece of his busy life on you. It was the basic working tool of the top grade confidence man.[68]

We meet two variations of the same pattern in Tom Pike *(The Girl in the Plain Brown Wrapper)* and Walter Demos *(The Dreadful Lemon Sky).* There is much of the glad-hander, wheeler-dealer in these men.

Far more chilling and much more dangerous, however, are the vicious, unfeeling villains whose perverse minds hide behind appealing, broad smiles. These villains are not sophisticated industrial developers or confidence people, operating for rational purposes. They are rather like spiders, whose smiles are shimmering webs, and who devour their snared prey bit by bit, at their own leisure. Junior Allen in *The Deep Blue Good-by* was the first. One of the heroines describes a scene where Allen sexually abused her, smiling all the while. Another says that when he beat her up, "hammering me there in the dark, nobody to hear, not caring if he killed me dead," she had gotten one quick look at his face—"and he was smiling." Finally, McGee lies awake at night, next to one of the women Allen had abused:

In my bed I thought of the brutal leathery hands of Junior Allen. Behind the agreeable grin he was as uncompromising as a hammer. Beast in his grin-mask. A clever, twisted thing, hunting for that perversion of innocence, the fornification of gentleness which would feed his own emptiness.[69]

In the fourth in the series, *The Quick Red Fox*, we meet Ulka Atlund M'Gruder, sweet, disarmingly beautiful, but deadly as a rattler. In *The Long Lavender Look*, McGee comes across some pornographic pictures of a woman (Lilo Perris) whose smile and "merry expression" can't hide a contradictory, harsh, "clamped-jaw resolve." Later on, McGee hears a story that bears out what he saw in the picture. A part-time hooker describes Lilo as a pimp's enforcer:

He sent Lilo to see me. That girl is crazy! She hurt me
so bad I fainted, I don't know how many times. After
she went away I kept throwing up. I was so weak I
stayed in bed two days. . . . I think I would rather die
than have her start doing things to me again, smiling at
me and giggling and calling me love names and saying
how much fun it would be to really kill me. She's as
strong as a man, and she knows every way there is to
hurt a girl. She's absolutely insane, Trav.[70]

The other two smiling killers are Boo Waxwell of *Bright
Orange for the Shroud* and Howie Brindle of *The Turquoise Lament.* Waxwell comes toward you, hand out-
stretched, cowboy hat tilted back, big smile, and when
you take his hand, kicks you swiftly in the kneecap, as
a prelude to stomping you into the ground. Brindle is
a big, lovable child-man who loves chocolate bars, and
who has murdered ten people. A smiling version of *The
Bad Seed* grown up undetected. The smiling killer is
hypocrisy at its deadliest. To be fooled by this pretense
is to face the villain with all defenses down—ultimately
to die, perhaps horribly. But what of the *villains* in
McGee's world?

What Is the Source of Evil?

In the Travis McGee Series, the villains fall roughly
into three categories.

The first, and most deadly, is the purely evil villain.
And McGee believes that such does exist, "that evil,
undiluted by any hint of childhood trauma, does exist in
the world, exists for its own precise sake."[71] These villains are pure sociopaths, nagged by no conscience, having no moral sense whatsoever. They lack all of the

basic humanizing emotions, love, guilt, pity, remorse, hate, despair, anger. They often experience a slight sexual stimulation from inflicting pain. They kill with no more involvement than a cow flicking a fly with her tail. Only occasionally does MacDonald make these characters stereotypical, like the ex-Nazi couple in *One Fearful Yellow Eye,* or the head-knocking corrupt cops, Freddy Hazard in *Pale Gray for Guilt* and King Sturnevan in *The Long Lavender Look.* For the most part these villains, both male and female, have no social-environmental explanation. They are virtually unrecognizable in conventional social settings, making them all the more dangerous. They do not look like evil people. They had neither a socially deprived upbringing nor cruel stepmothers who beat them into repressed hostility. They are evil, and purely so. The smiling killers fall into this category.

The second group of villains in the McGee series we call the "industrialist manipulator." This villain is not purely evil, but evil for a purpose. That is, the evil in this villain is not incarnate (satanic); rather, evil results flow from this man's avarice. (I say "man" because the six or seven examples of this type in the series are all men.) All these villains are wealthy, and interested solely in stockpiling and expanding that wealth, at anyone else's expense. They are not all industrialists—some are lawyers or politicians. But MacDonald draws attention to the exploitation of the land by developers, mostly in his native Florida, so "industrialist manipulator" covers fairly well.

This category is more fluid than the first. Only Gary Santo in *Pale Gray for Guilt,* Tom Collier in *The Turquoise Lament,* and Baynard Mulligan in *Nightmare in*

Pink fit this classification strictly. Calvin Tomberlin in
A Deadly Shade of Gold and Fred Van Harn in *The
Dreadful Lemon Sky* combine the wealthy manipulator with lustful interest in kinky sex (more typical of the
purely evil villain). In *The Girl in the Plain Brown
Wrapper,* MacDonald presents a purely evil villain who
is also an industrial manipulator (Tom Pike). And in
Bright Orange for the Shroud, a professional confidence man is also a wealthy manipulator villain.

The third type of villain is the least deadly. We call
him the "semi-corrupt middle person." These villains
are in league with villains of types one and two, but they
are neither evil in themselves nor are they wealthy.
They are more manipulated than manipulators. Caught
in an evil web of circumstances which they only partly
caused, they have become inextricably entangled. Consequently, they are weak, vulnerable people, and as
such they serve the plot well. McGee ferrets them out,
terrorizes them with physical force or blackmail to
break them down, and with their cooperation flushes
out the more dangerous villains of types one and two.
This semi-corrupt middle person is present in every
novel, with the exception of *The Scarlet Ruse* and *The
Turquoise Lament.* In the face of all this evil, who can
possibly save us?

What Is the Source of the Good?

Who can conquer such villains and so rescue the
townspeople? Travis McGee, of course, is our deliverer.
McGee is a semiretired beach bum who lives on a spec-
tacular houseboat in Bahia Mar, Fort Lauderdale,
Florida. He earns his living by working, no more than

six months of the year, to help people recover large sums of money at a fee of half of what is recovered. His philosophy is, if they have none, they will be overjoyed to have half, and happy to give him the other half. As it happens, things never quite work out that way, though he almost always ends up with enough to finance another six months of his retirement. These book-cover excerpts highlight his best-selling attributes:

—that big, loose-jointed boat bum, that slayer of small savage fish, that beach walker, gin drinker, quip-maker

—soldier of fortune, thinking man's Robin Hood, a man who works just this side of the law to make a living stealing from thieves

—that big, loose, chaser of rainbows

—slayer of dragons, savior of lily-white maidens

—amiable and incurable tilter at conformity, boat bum Quixote, hopeless sucker for starving kittens, women in distress, and large, loose sums of money

—that intrepid savior of ladies in distress, the free-lance knight whose armor covers a heart of 14-karat gold

How does Travis McGee help us? For the more ambiguous problems he has less satisfying solutions, but more consistent ones. He exposes and refuses to respect hypocrisy; he punctures the blowhard balloons of all sorts of people. He is no respecter of professional position, social status, or wealth. In this way he continually

demonstrates how we hide from ourselves and use
these social devices as fronts. He rumbles like a prophet
on every ecological issue. Most significant to the plot of
any particular book, McGee restores the social balance.
He gets the money back, drives the murderer to a just
fate, makes the industrialist manipulator pay for his
sins. When he confronts pure evil incarnate in a showdown scene, he destroys it.

Although these activities may in fact restore the *social* balance, McGee does not believe that society itself
can be redeemed. There is no "answer," no final resolution for the whole, for the social world. McGee's destruction of evil may benefit society, but he intends to
bring justice or satisfaction only to some particular individual:

I know just enough about myself to know I cannot settle
for one of the simplifications which indignant people
seize upon to make understandable a world too complex for their comprehension. Astrology, health food,
flag waving, Bible thumping, Zen, nudism, nihilism—all
of these are grotesque simplifications which small
dreary people adopt in the hope of thereby finding The
Answer, because the very concept that maybe there is
no answer, never has been, never will be, terrifies them.
. . . All that remains for the McGee is an ironic Knight-
hood, a spavined steed, second class armor, a dubious
lance, a bent broadsword, and the chance, now and
again, to lift into a galumphing charge against capital E
Evil. . . . He has to carry a very long banner because on
it is embroidered . . . The Only Thing in the World
Worth a Damn Is the Strange, Touching, Pathetic, Awesome Nobility of the Individual Human Spirit.[72]

McGee not only wipes out the source of the particular evil plaguing the individual person, but very often engages in restoring the damaged person to personal health. He saves the victimized person from the villain *and* from the more general conditions of evil in the society as a whole. In theological terms, the victim's "justification" is the defeat of the purely evil villain or the industrialist-manipulator villain. The additional process of restoration and personal fulfillment is the victim's "sanctification." McGee does not do this latter task as "empowered savior"; rather he does it as "mediating priest." Life itself bears a restorative power about which McGee knows, upon which he draws, and in which he truly and completely believes. It is the life-invigorating power of the health of the natural physical body. It is, if we could give it a philosophical tag, McGee's "naturalism."

Often, the way McGee's own special instincts and abilities focus this naturalism appears when he must react quickly to the presence of evil. He continually notes in his bodily reactions an animal preparedness necessary to survival.

I stood in the night, listening, and felt my nostrils widen. Another atavistic reflex . . . readying the muscles, blood, brain, for that explosive effort necessary for survival in a jungle of predators.[73]

Once when McGee's mind and emotions had been clouded by a particularly luscious villain, it is finally his body that warns him about what his mind will not accept. Travis McGee, paragon of virility, goes limp and cannot perform. Later he discovers the meaning of his impotence:

But last night some strange kind of survival instinct had taken over. The body seems to have its own awareness of the realities. In the churny night, the tangly bed, abaft that resilient everlasting smorgasbord, body-knowledge said "Whoa!" And Whoa it was, abruptly. One just doesn't do this sort of thing with monsters. Not with a plastic monster which would kill you on any whim if it was certain it would never be caught, and if it anticipated being amused by the experience.[74]

The more usual function of this naturalism of his physical body is a kind of life-affirming sexual sanctification. Every book features either a wounded-bird syndrome, where McGee nurses a young lady back to health and happiness, or a physical sex relationship that affirms life in the face of death. Some books have both. McGee is willing on occasion to sleep with women with whom he has no close relationship, violating one of his own basic principles, so great is the need to assert life when death and despair creep upon one's horizon. In *A Deadly Shade of Gold,* McGee telephones a beach bunny whose sexual advances he had just recently scorned on principle:

I felt the brute rejection of my apartness in this world, of too many losses and too few gains, of too much of the dirty underside of things, of too much vulnerability. It had all the sour tang of that post-coital depression which occurs when something hasn't meant enough. On the floor of my mind splintered mahogany floated in the puddled metallic blood. . . . I put a robe on and let the Junebug number ring once before I hung up. I left the door ajar and sat in the dark living room. She pushed the door open cautiously and said, "Was that you?" And she was a warmth to cling to, to keep from drowning.[75]

In *The Turquoise Lament,* McGee has a similar liaison with a nurse:

"There are so many *old* ones coming in, coming in and *dying* all the time. . . . They don't know what is happening, and then all of a sudden they're in a coma and they got an I.V. going, and a catheter and a bag, and an oxygen clip on their nose, and they don't know a damn thing about living or dying anymore. That's going to be me and you sometime, bet on it." . . . In about ten minutes we were on the mattress together. . . . Thus we exorcized our private ghosts, leaving *old* and *dying* far behind as sensation rushed forward in the rich, frictive celebration of life and living.[76]

Still, life affirmation is best when shared within a caring, ongoing relationship, between two people who are willing to commit more than body. At the end of *Dress Her in Indigo,* after McGee has met and dealt with an incredible assortment of predatory villains and insensitive manipulators, he restores his faith in life-reality with Elana, a Mexican girl of "a splendid earthiness spiced with innocent wonder"—the perfectly natural woman, uninhibited by complex social rationalizations.

So with gray at the windows, and her mouth turning upward for the kiss, with the slow deep steady beat that would begin to change only when we neared climax, *this* became the reality, *this* became the life-moment, *this* became the avowal, the communion, the immortality. The private rhythm of our need, a small and personal and totally shared thing.[77]

The book ends two lines later. Even deliverer-hero Travis McGee is linked with the American mythic belief, already pointed to in the Western and in country music especially, that women are the source of grace. Restored in spirit by Elana, McGee exclaims: "Bless all the sisters, wherever they are."

What Is Salvation?

What are the characteristics of the fully restored and happy situation, of fulfillment? We have already seen what the elements of the fulfilled situation *must* be in this belief system. We need only briefly summarize them.

Restored Social Balance

Essential are the defeat or annihilation of the villain, the return of the stolen goods, the social humiliation or ruin of the manipulator and corrupt middle person. But note: The anti-Western social view of detective fiction undermines any eschatological possibilities in such an ending. There is no new heaven and new earth, no redeemed social world. There is only restoration of the precariously balanced, still-polluted, overly structured, plastic and phony world. The newness, the fulfillment, the life-enriching salvation is only experienced personally, between two people, and possibly by their small group of friends. The world as a whole remains unchanged, unchangeable. But people can find each other within it.

Retribution

There is the satisfaction of having rendered just retribution, an eye for an eye. Cruel villains meet cruel fates, the punishment often fits the crime. McGee accepts the necessity of this justice. Part of being restored to health is this satisfaction. This very American emotion is inhibited every time a "known criminal" goes free because of a "technicality" in the law. The Old and New Testaments sometimes support this kind of justice as necessary to a satisfactory salvation, especially in the apocalyptic sections of Revelation.

Physical Health and Well-being

A good healthy body assures a good healthy mind. Often the "wounded birds" McGee tries to help are drowning in their own intellectual or socially conditioned hang-ups. All McGee does is short-circuit their rationalizations with blunt honesty and give their bodies fresh air, good food, and rigorous exercise. When they are so tired they forget to rationalize, their natural physical reflexes take over. The wisdom of the body is its own source of healing grace. And when the treatment is over, the wounded bird is ready to return to the world:

The next day I had cast off and gone chugging down to the Keys bearing my wan, huddled, jittery passenger. Three weeks later I delivered her to the Miami airport for her flight back. She was ten pounds heavier, brown as walnuts, her hair bleached three shades lighter, her hands toughened by rowing, her muscles toned and springy. We kissed the long humid goodbys and she laughed and cried—not in hysterics, but because she had good reasons for laughing and good reasons for crying, and we both knew just how she could pick up the pieces of her life and build something that would make sense.[78]

What Is the Way?

What is left for the saved one, the disciple, to do to complete the process of fulfillment? For the characters in the book, not much. They go forth to lead reconstituted lives as best they can. They have learned from McGee and have been healed by him. But the series is not concerned with this, for one important reason. The dominant value system (the resolution of the social problem) and the subdominant value system (the resolution of the personal problem) cross at the image of humanity found in Travis McGee himself. Whereas for the former system McGee is the deliverer, for the latter system McGee is salvation itself. He *is* the image of fulfilled humanity found in the book. Therefore, the Way is followed by the readers, fans who devour book after book, reading them each again and again. We may not be able to change the world, but we can rearrange our personal space. McGee is the model. He says of a character in *The Dreadful Lemon Sky:* "She wanted a good life. It is not an unusual hope, but a very unusual attainment." We have the same hope. This is one of the main reasons we read Travis McGee.

8

Implications for the Church

So what? All this was entertaining, you say. But, so what? We can hardly afford to leave the impression that what we are about is merely entertainment. If you want that, you can *go* to a movie instead of reading about one. We have maintained from the beginning that this endeavor was not only of interest to Christians, but crucially important to them. Something more than light, fictional fun and games is going on in American popular culture. It is something vital to any Christian who is concerned about the state of his or her own Christian self-understanding, something vital to any Christian concerned about the difficult task of helping others to find Jesus Christ. But all we have given so far are some categories and a ton and a half of observations to go in them. We would be far less than responsible, and we would be undermining the whole purpose of this book, if we did not attempt to pull this material together toward some future use. To this task this final chapter will be devoted.

Two preliminary issues must be raised. First, by way of lowering anticipation and reducing disappointment, we should say that the implications of this study for a theological understanding of what it means to be a

Christian in contemporary America are more extensive and complicated than we can probe. We can barely raise the questions here. The interface of the dominant and subdominant American belief systems with the Christian understanding of humanity, community, evil, innocence, salvation, and divine power and justice will be the subject of a later study. Secondly, this qualification in no way prevents us from urging Christian clergy and laity to prompt, deliberate, and specific action. We will deal directly in this chapter with what *you* can begin to *do*, not tomorrow, or next year, or after another study comes out, but *now*. To stimulate some concrete response is the whole motivating purpose of this book. Therefore, we can hardly conclude without making suggestions to that end.

First, we will review the theological rationale for the study and our major theses. Second, we will summarize categorically the major cultural themes we have uncovered, and point to their significant issues. Finally, we will indicate some steps toward the development of Christian self-understanding which this type of analysis can assist.

RATIONALES AND THESES

There are at least two reasons why the study of popular culture is a significant responsibility for American Christians. First, when we dismiss as irrelevant any area of our life together as human beings, we are denying the sovereign presence of God. To meet God in our daily lives we have to be willing to develop and grow in that one characteristic of Christian humanness to which Calvin pointed so adamantly, hearing. One of the

reasons that we so often think God isn't answering our
prayers is that we have so limited his access to us that
we have become deaf to his voice. But Christ told us
that he is present to us in our neighbor; and we know
that God speaks to us more often in the midst of this life
than through oracles, priests, and Scriptures, though we
will need these to be able to distinguish God's voice
from its human messenger. Our stance before God
should be as listeners. We may be surprised to hear him
speak to us through a film or a song or a television
program, but we should at least be embarrassed to have
been so confident we would not hear him.

Our second reason for urging Christians to become
familiar with popular culture has to do with communication. Most people to whom we speak about the gospel
couldn't care less. Even those who are interested seem
to be so little affected by this story about Jesus in their
everyday lives that we get discouraged. The problem is
the same in both situations. We know the message is
important, that the issues touched by the gospel are
life-and-death issues. Do people not care about life and
death? Surely they do. But they already have their questions answered. They are already operating on the basis
of functioning beliefs about life and death, about good
and evil, about who they are and the purpose of life.
They may not be Hindus or Buddhists, but they might
as well be for our purposes. An American already has a
"religious" commitment, a religious belief system, simply from growing up in American society. Until persons
are able to challenge their unthinking (or thinking) acceptance of the American cultural value system, they
will either not hear what we tell them about the gospel,
or they will translate what we say into their already

functioning system of beliefs. Although we may teach and preach the gospel every week, we have only limited time at most when the game is played by Christian rules. The rest of the week, as the people participate in the popular culture entertainment, this worship liturgy of the American cultural religion is reaffirming their cultural belief system with a repetition and force with which the Christian church cannot possibly compete.

Our major thesis has been that popular culture is to what Americans believe as worship services are to what people in institutional religions believe. Popular culture is not nonsense, simply because it is not art. Art (theater, great literature, classical music, the graphic arts, and such) challenges one's self-understanding toward self-criticism and insight, raising the possibility that one may choose new options. The primary function of the ritual of worship services is to affirm already-held beliefs and values, not to suggest different options. We would be greatly surprised to find that a Christian believer had been converted to Hinduism through a Christian worship service. Popular culture, besides being entertainment, is a dramatic ritual enactment of the dominant and subdominant American cultural belief systems. It is where Americans worship, where they get their values reinforced, whether they know it or not. As Christian Americans, this revelation should prompt some self-evaluation. It may wake us up to the real values of popular culture from the Christian point of view. If we need to find out what Americans believe in their already active cultural religion, and those beliefs and values are being dramatically paraded for us in popular culture media, then popular culture could be the key to more effective communication of the gospel in American society. We will not only know where our own and other persons' real values lie, but we will begin to get some idea what modes of presentation and what kinds of illustrations might be most effective in getting across our message.

SUMMARY OF MAJOR THEMES AND ISSUES IN THE AMERICAN BELIEF SYSTEMS

We have two initial qualifications. First, we comprehensively portrayed the major categories of the dominant American belief system in their usual dramatic form through our analysis of the "Western" in Chapter 2. That exposition is basic because these categories are still formative in American life. Second, the anti-Western movement of popular dissent from these classic categories may be peaking, as trends toward nostalgic classical romanticism and simplistic solutions hark back to more optimistic days. But anti-Western sentiment is not dismissed by wishful thinking. For twenty years its doubts have dogged our footsteps. The impact has been profound and deep; all the hopeful rhetoric of the newly revived classic system cannot erase such marks. We must be sensitive in the Western character of the themes we will now mention to the anti-Western underside.

We found that a central value in American self-understanding was some form of satisfying interpersonal relations, a form of community most often identified with the family. Here "family" functions as an ideal kind of community. It involves the values of loyalty, equality of membership, love, and a purpose in and of the fellowship itself. But however ideal, the family most representative of these values in the American belief system is the nuclear family, husband, wife, and probably children. In the classic Western form, the identification is complete. The wife/mother is the center of civilization itself, standing for schools, churches, and the like, while providing the means of domesticating the male and making him responsible. The country-music version of the adult human problem can be categorized as threats to this same family-community. It represents the wife/mother as the source of grace, bearing such an essential goodness that her occasional "fallenness" always has external causes—it is not her fault. One variety of woman's magazine (the *Ladies' Home Journal* type) connects the fulfillment of individual female identity necessarily with the same family-community. Television situation comedies *(Father Knows Best, The Donna Reed Show)* used to make the same assumption, and occasionally still do, but with more recognizably sociopolitical implications *(All in the Family, Maude)*. Dramatically, *The Waltons* has made a fortune with the same identification. Soap operas and romance magazines don't deal as much with the form of family-community itself, though both necessarily presuppose it for credibility purposes. Even in the citified Western form, the detective story, with its gloomy anti-Western mood, the male-female relationship not only survives (though possibly not in marriage) but is found to possess healing power when all else fails.

The value of the individual in the American self-understanding has always had positive, though occasionally anti-Western, connotations. Power to resolve and transform situations effectively is seen to reside in the individual, rather than in the community. The deliverer-hero has always represented this in the American belief system. The resolved situation was classically a social one, however, linking the individual's resourceful power to social ends. The sacrifice of the individual is *for* the community, rather than for himself, and receives its sacred meaning from the essential innocence of the community. The meaning of fulfilled individuality is found in serving the good by protecting it from evil. Thus, when the community is revealed to be less than the good it was supposed to be, as in the anti-Western, the sacrifice of the individual begins to lose its redemptive and fulfilling meaning. The community must be worth the sacrifice. It is easily understandable that a version of the sacrifice of Jesus Christ which portrays humanity as the essentially innocent victim of satanic powers would be popular with American Christians. The gospel, of course, says exactly the opposite. Far from being essentially innocent, humanity not only was not worth the sacrifice, and didn't want it anyway, but was also responsible for Jesus' death—and would be anytime he came!

The nonfamily male or female individual is considered potentially a troublemaker, a destroyer of value and community, except in the eligible male or future-homemaker role. The nonfamily female means available sexual satisfaction outside the marriage relationship, and temptation to the married male who, being adolescent, would prefer "easy lovin'" to responsible love. The nonfamily male perpetuates the male camaraderie fantasies that formerly shaped and controlled the now-married male's self-understanding. The unmarried male is thus a threat to the family as a lure to the married male, and as a sign of the casual freedom of a masculine life-style which makes the male-female family seem oppressive by comparison.

The male community traditionally has been the only form of community not family-based. Formerly, the outlaw gang represented this possibility. Since the male community maintains those values which have always made wars both possible and inevitable, military forms of male community have always been acceptable to the family-community. The content Western idealizes this tendency through the cavalry. More recently, the anti-Western has been the vehicle for a reverence-for-the-outlaw resurgence of male-male camaraderie forms of interpersonal relations, both as studies of the male community and its standards *(The Wild Bunch)*, and as a corporate form of the deliverer-hero *(The Sting, M*A*S*H)*. The truck driver mythos in country music, where formerly the truck driver was the idealized, powerful, and mobile individual personified, has more recently appeared as a celebration of male camaraderie as maintained through the citizen's band radio (reaching apocalyptic proportions in C. W. McCall's "Convoy"). Although we did not survey professional sports, the Vince Lombardi professional football team value system is another striking example of the resurgence of male community as a value-determining social form. The male hunting and fishing community as represented in the barbershop magazines continues to be popular enough to maintain the sales of these magazines, even though these magazines portray a version of male-female relations that is more characteristic of a former time in American cultural history.

We also noted the rising popularity of two challenges to the family-community and male-community life-styles. One is the sisterhood community advocated by *Ms.* magazine, which like the more traditional male community often views the opposite sex as a threat to healthy interpersonal relations. The other option, formerly restricted to hero-deliverer figures, is the cool, sophisticated, self-sufficient individual of *Playboy* and *Cosmopolitan.* This individual is fulfilled *without* community of any kind. Appropriately enough, the country-music version of this development is the "cowboy" mythos, represented in personalities like Waylon Jennings and Willie Nelson. We find it in songs like Ed Bruce's rendition of "Mamas Don't Let Your Babies Grow Up to Be Cowboys"; in fashion by boots and pearl-studded Western shirts. (The Ed Bruce song describes the "cowboy" life-style so appealingly that the song title itself is mocked!)

One other interesting tension in the family-community American belief system merits particular attention. As we have argued throughout, the husband-wife "family" is a microcosm of the society at large. We are meant to understand this in ritual drama. This is the reason we have no difficulty seeing the same values represented in *Ladies' Home Journal,* country music, and *The Waltons,* on the one hand; and in *M*A*S*H, The Mary Tyler Moore Show, The Rookies,* and *Police Woman* on the other. In tension with this, however, is the anti-Western thrust of detective fiction, particularly that form represented in the Raymond Chandler–John D. MacDonald (Travis McGee) tradition. For Travis McGee, the male-female unit is fundamental to life's meaning; it may even be redemptive. But it is seldom the same microcosm of society that the more traditional male-female, family-community model presents. In fact, the McGee "family" unit of male-female is more often anti-society, in that all other societal groups are corrupt and dehumanizing. We see in McGee's "community" not what ideally might be possible for the whole society, but what is *never* possible for society as a whole or for its institutions (e.g., marriage).

There are many other cultural threads in this material, but it was never our intention to spell them all out. However, let us highlight one more before we turn to specific suggestions for programmatic continuation of this study in the local church situation. The tendency of the American belief system is always to identify the source of evil as external to the community itself. This is true in the Western form, in country music, in popular magazines, in television, and even in detective fiction. Even when everybody lives in the same community (the city), it always turns out that those people responsible for the suffering of the community were not human in the same way as other good and innocent members of the community. Therefore, when these villains are violently annihilated, we experience satisfaction. They certainly deserved what they got. This view is strongly reinforced within popular culture. It may be the main reason Americans generally cannot feel empathy for the "criminal element," and accounts as well for the popularity of capital punishment. Those we throw in jail for life, and those we execute, are not members of our family-community. People who feel this way are not themselves perverse, or evil, or sadomasochistic. Rather they are sinners like you and me, whose way of perceiving other human beings is more shaped by American cultural values than by the God of grace whose forgiveness is manifest in the Christ of the Gospels; a Christ who died, between thieves, on a cross *for* sinners. It should be obvious that discussions within the church on issues like capital punishment and crime in America are hopeless, unless American Christians have the opportunity to raise critical questions about the necessary connection of justice and violence, and the simplistic distinction between good (community) and bad (source of evil), with which we have all grown up.

THINGS TO DO AND THINK ABOUT

1. Remember these two points about popular culture in America:

a. Resist the temptation to dismiss it as trivial. Aesthetically, it may be worthless. But it is far more informative of what we believe as Americans than "art" or "high culture" could ever be. Whether or not we approve of it, popular culture is not going to go away. Lamenting television as a "wasteland" and shunning its clichés and "low" humor for the climate of the Public Broadcasting System may be satisfying to your ego, but satisfying your ego may not be what Jesus had in mind. The same holds true for detective fiction, country music, and popular magazines—as well as for professional sports. Clichés like "trash" and "hillbilly" are forms of blindness that can only build walls between Christian Americans.

b. Popular culture is ritual drama; it is not everyday life. The policeman who shoots down the fleeing criminal may have to face a due-process investigation. But we would be shocked into disbelief if the townspeople arrested the hero-deliverer for the same reasons, after he had shot the villain. To show a film like *Walking Tall,* and then to ask the question, "What would I have done as a Christian if I lived in that town during these events?" is a misunderstanding of what is going on in the film. The events of the film may be taken from the "true life story" of Sheriff Buford Pusser, but the *impact* of the film from a belief-systems point of view is the same, whether these events ever really happened or not.

2. The intent of this study is not to force Christians to choose between being Christians and being Americans. We are both, as long as we live in this country and claim Jesus Christ as Lord and Savior. It will never be different, nor should it be. But "being an American" is a certain way of seeing and valuing life. At times it is essentially the same as that way of seeing and valuing life which we call Christian. We should recognize and point to these interfaces. But we should also be especially aware of those issues, such as the external nature of evil, on which these belief systems have strong disagreement. Pointing out these issues could help people see more clearly what is particularly distinctive about "being a Christian."

3. Keep your fingers on the pulse of the American value system. Continue to develop the sensitizing process which it is hoped this study has begun. The value system is changing. If our ministry is going to be effective, we have to "keep up" on those particular issues within the American self-understanding to which the gospel could most easily speak.

This can be done in two ways. First, as individuals we need to tune in on popular culture, being particularly aware of the value level, or the ritual drama, being performed. This requires a standing back from the pull of the details of the drama, and a watchful waiting for recognizable value assertions. Secondly, as members of groups within the church, hold continuing workshops on popular cultural materials, first to raise consciousness in the group itself, and then to continue the "fingers on the pulse" task. For instance, take some popular magazines and cut out symbolic references to various male and female life-styles, and build a collage for each type of magazine. When a television show of a new type becomes popular, assign everybody to watch it for a month. Then get together for a final viewing at someone's house, and talk about the values making the show popular. The incredible success of shows like *Welcome Back, Kotter* and *Happy Days* with high-school-age young people bears investigation. Rent films that are American classics or that are extremely popular, or both, and focus discussion of societal values on the film's ritual drama. In our experience, discussion leaders for film programs are absolutely necessary. These "leaders" should always preview the film once or twice before the group showing, to give the mind a chance to absorb the belief-system material, and to prevent their becoming too wrapped up in the plot.

4. Be responsible for what *you* believe. Recognizing the characteristics of the American belief system is only one half of the task. One can hardly be critical, whether positive or negative, of values from a neutral position. There *is* a Christian value system, a Christian belief system. We should all have some idea what its premises are. The lack of understanding of this has always been partially the fault of the church's theologians, whose theology is written mostly for scholars, and on occasion can put even them to sleep. Every Christian lay person

should be responsible for understanding and being able
to articulate to others exactly what the Christian message is about. What is the Christian understanding of
"community"? What is the Christian understanding of
being individually "male" and "female"? Does the
church see the "family-community" as a microcosm of
the ideal community? Has the cultural identification of
family so captured the church's own self-understanding
that the church finds it impossible to direct its ministry
to the divorced, separated, or single-parent family?
What is the Christian view of justice? of righteousness?
of sin? of the sources of good and evil? It is hoped the
study of the American cultural belief systems will stimulate interest in and concern for asking these theological
questions.

This approach will not only renew interest in Christian theology but will also enable clergy and lay people
to determine their logical priorities. Those theological
issues whose study will most quickly spill over into relevant life application will virtually leap out at us from
our study of the American cultural belief system. In this
way, the theological issues that we spend time investi-
gating will arise *in* active ministry, in concern for those
particular frustrations and anxieties now enveloping us
and our neighbors. And the agenda of doing theology in
the church will be set by our having given first place in
the life of the church to Jesus' commandment: "All authority in heaven and on earth has been given to me.
Go therefore and make disciples of all nations, baptiz-
ing them in the name of the Father and of the Son and
of the Holy Spirit, teaching them to observe all that I
have commanded you" (Matthew 28:18–20).

Notes

1. Cyclops, *The New York Times*, Arts and Leisure Section, Feb. 24, 1974, p. 15.

2. What follows is dependent on the following sources in the following ways: The sections on setting, women, corrupt townspeople, on John G. Cawelti, *The Six-Gun Mystique.* The section on villains, on Cawelti. The section on heroes mainly on Robert Warshow, partly on Homans and Cawelti. The section on good, evil, and violence, on Cawelti and Homans. The Homans source is his much reprinted article, "Puritanism Revisited: An Analysis of the Contemporary Screen-Image Western," as it appears in *Focus on the Western*, ed. by Jack Nachbar, pp. 84–92. The Warshow source is the famous essay, "Movie Chronicle: The Westerner," from his book *The Immediate Experience*, reprinted just about everywhere, and also in Nachbar, pp. 45–56.

3. Cawelti, p. 36.

4. The word "he" is used intentionally here, rather than as a result of unconscious male chauvinism. In the Western form, heroes and villains are always male.

5. Cawelti, pp. 14, 19.

6. This section is heavily dependent on Cawelti, pp. 46–66. The material on the hero is dependent, as indicated in note 2 above, on Warshow.

7. Cawelti, p. 47.

8. See discussion immediately below.

9. See Chapter 7. Also, Robert Warshow, "The Gangster as Tragic Hero," in *The Immediate Experience*, reprinted

among other places in *Things in the Driver's Seat: Readings in Popular Culture,* ed. by Harry Russell Huebel, pp. 97–102.

10. Cawelti, pp. 52–53.

11. "Movie Chronicle: The Westerner," in Nachbar, p. 46.

12. *Ibid.,* p. 54.

13. *Ibid.,* pp. 54–55.

14. It will be interesting to see if *Playboy*'s sales drop off concurrent with revived interest in the classic Western form.

15. Especially *Public Enemy,* with James Cagney, and *Little Caesar* with Edward G. Robinson.

16. It will be obvious to those who remember the United States of the early 1950's that *Bad Day at Black Rock* is "about" the anti-Communist hysteria of the McCarthy hearings. The sociopolitical intentions of the film are not, however, our chief concern.

17. E.g., hero Tracy arrives and departs on a train, a feature of the classic Western raised to symbolic pose by John Ford's films. The sheriff cannot bring law and order to the community. On his visit to the jail Tracy finds Sheriff Dean Jagger sleeping off a drunken binge in one of his own cells! Tracy's final act of violence is thereby justified according to standard Western form. Tracy displays all the traditional "Cool" of the deliverer-hero, turning to violence only when absolutely forced to so do. Tracy has, as well, a mysterious background —typical of the deliverer-hero. Though the villains are members of the community, they are still distinguished from the really good community members who have merely been led astray by their evil leaders. Two of these "leaders" are played by Lee Marvin and Ernest Borgnine, stock Hollywood villain examples of sloppy, wholeheartedly violent characters.

18. The only cast rivaling *The Professionals* is *The Magnificent Seven,* starring Yul Brynner, Steve McQueen, James Coburn, Charles Bronson, Robert Vaughn, and Eli Wallach.

19. The film ends in a freeze frame before they are killed. Thus, we see them "immortalized."

20. There may be some debate on this point. For instance, she may have slept with Redford to keep track of him; or director George Roy Hill may have had the spider analogy in mind, i.e., that the female devours the male after they have

had sexual relations. I prefer my own interpretation.

21. See the excellent article by Ralph Brauer, "Who Are Those Guys? The Movie Western During the TV Era," in Nachbar, pp. 118–128.

22. The definitive article on this subject, and one upon which we are dependent, is Gary Engle, *"McCabe and Mrs. Miller:* Robert Altman's Anti-Western," in *The Journal of Popular Culture,* Vol. I, No. 4 (Fall 1972), pp. 268–287. Engle's analysis is near-perfect, though he doesn't operate with an interpretive structure or model of interpretation sufficient to do his insights full justice.

23. Cf. Jack Nachbar, "Riding Shotgun: The Scattered Formula in Contemporary Western Movies," in Nachbar, p. 107.

24. John Ford, as we might have expected, first symbolized the gathering at the church as indicative of the community-as-come-of-age in the now-famous dance at the half-built church scene in *My Darling Clementine,* 1946.

25. Engle, pp. 273–274.

26. Cf. Engle, pp. 274–275; Nachbar, p. 111; Brauer, p. 126; and Charles Baker, "The Theme of Structure in the Films of Robert Altman," in *The Journal of Popular Film,* Vol. II, No. 3 (Summer 1973), p. 256.

27. Brauer, p. 126.

28. See Chapter 2.

29. Of course, Shane rides off into the sunset. But just before he leaves, as he stops his horse to speak with Joey (Brandon de Wilde), we discover that he was wounded in the shoot-out, and is now bleeding profusely from a stomach wound. As he rides off, we see him slump slightly in the saddle. We know he is mortally wounded, since we know his messianic deliverance of the community is sacrificial. But we do not see him die. Butch Cassidy and Sundance receive the same treatment in the film of the same name, and so does Davy Crockett in Disney's version of the story.

30. Noted in Engle, p. 276.

31. Engle, p. 286.

32. My attention was drawn to this film by Professor Robert Ezzell of Pittsburgh Theological Seminary, to whose unpublished paper "Walking Tall: Buford Pusser as American Mes-

siah," I owe some of these ideas. Professor Ezzell's paper, however, is on a slightly different subject, i.e., the co-opting of Christian motifs and symbols by *Walking Tall.*

33. Rhythm and blues, or "soul" music, is very popular in this country, but it is not popular only with adults, nor is it *about* subjects that are especially a part of adult life. Soul is popular with teen-agers, as well as with adults, and its subject matter is equally applicable to both groups. Country music may be popular with some teen-agers, but its audience is almost entirely post-teen-age, or at least post-high school, and so is its subject matter. Jazz is not really popular music, nor is Dixieland. The structure of the former is too close to that of classical music, limiting the potential of its appeal to a small group of devotees. Dixieland is popular in some parts of the country, but its influence is not far-flung. Most significantly jazz and Dixieland are both mainly instrumental—greatly limiting their possible focus as liturgical for the cultural belief system. Soul music, on the other hand, might be excellent material for analyzing belief systems among American blacks, since it is mainly their music and tells us a lot about where they have been (e.g., Cone). The problem with such an endeavor will be separating adult belief-system answers from pre-adult or adolescent belief-system assertions. The latter are troublesome, as we have said, because they tend to be intermixed with particularly pre-adult problems, such as self-identity, or youthful idealism vs. adult realism seen as duplicity. For these same reasons, I will treat here neither soul nor rock music. The latter is fundamentally pre-marriage, family, work responsibilities, and is often greatly preoccupied with the introspection and the same identity problems previously mentioned. Both of these concerns continue without the tension of "life-lost," or "I'm trapped" frustrations. Those rock songs that do deal with these issues are very "heavy," and philosophical truths and truisms are too form-shattering to support ritual drama. Still, those whose work is primarily with youth, or whose concerns are there, could easily use the belief-systems approach to do an analysis of what is ritually being reaffirmed for adolescents in the most popular rock music. All these generalizations to the wind, however, here country mu-

sic—the only uniquely adult, successfully popular form of music in American life—will be our subject.

34. This theme is prominently treated in Paul Ricoeur's *The Symbolism of Evil.*

35. How about Johnny Cash? someone will say. Certainly many of his songs have been very sharply biting social comments—on subjects that country-music people have found hard to swallow. But Cash combines folk, country, and pop; he would have an audience even if a large majority of country-music fans turned against him. This is not true of Hall. He depends primarily upon country-music audiences for his support, and would not be a star without the good faith of country-music fans.

36. Cyclops, "On Deep-Sixing Sitcom Characters," *The New York Times,* Sunday, March 30, 1975, p. 23.

37. Maryann Brinley, "Fathers and Daughters," *Ladies' Home Journal,* Nov. 1974, p. 124.

38. Stephanie Harrington, "Two Faces of the Same Eve: *Ms.* versus *Cosmo,*" *The New York Times Magazine,* Aug. 11, 1974, p. 10. The figures that follow are taken from Ms. Harrington's article.

39. Angela Lambert, "In Praise of Casanova," *Cosmopolitan,* Oct. 1974, p. 24.

40. Avery Corman, "The Beginning of the End of Sex: The First Baby," *Cosmopolitan,* Oct. 1974, p. 219.

41. Harrington, *loc. cit.*

42. Ellen Willis, "To Be or Not to Be a Mother . . . ," *Ms.,* Oct. 1974, pp. 28–36.

43. Formative for the following is the excellent article by W. Gerson and S. H. Lund, "*Playboy* Magazine: Sophisticated Smut or Social Revolution?" *The Journal of Popular Culture,* Vol. I, No. 3 (Winter 1967).

44. "Naturalistic" means in this context the assertion of the natural-physical as superior to the rational-mental in providing fulfillment. E.g., touching and holding is better than talking about it; feeling is better than thinking. "Relativistic" means drawing the principles of one's behavior from the context of the situation rather than from some trans-situation norms of moral behavior. The "libertarian rightists" (e.g., Ayn

Rand, Robert Heinlein, William F. Buckley) support maximum individual liberties in any situation not harmful to others, and are strongly against any form of big government. They perceive the latter to be .overstepping its bounds in interfering with a person's private life, e.g., snooping, keeping files on people.

45. This section is indebted in part to an excellent article by David Sonerschein, "Love and Sex in the Romance Magazines," *The Journal of Popular Culture*, Vol. IV, No. 2 (Fall 1970).

46. The author is grateful to Dr. Steven Polley for his research in this area.

47. This section is based on William Kuhns, *The Electronic Gospel.*

48. Kuhns, p. 30.

49. See above, Chapters 1 and 2.

50. The types of communities represented by the Mafia, the gun-toting mamma and her brood, the Indians, *et al.*, are all demonstrably perverse, according to the American belief system. Mafia members kill each other off without much compassion. Only when the Mafia gang itself is the hero of a film (e.g., *The Godfather*) is their community basis sympathetically treated. The gun-toting mamma is a family dictator to sniveling, stupid sons. The Indians, well, they are savages anyway, in their role as villains.

51. Carol Traynor Williams, "It's Not so Much, 'You've come a long way, Baby'—As You're Gonna Make It After All," in *The Journal of Popular Culture*, Vol. VII, No. 4 (Spring 1974), p. 988.

52. Our analysis is based on Anthony Astrachan, "Life Can Be Beautiful/Relevant," *The New York Times Magazine*, March 23, 1975, p. 12; and Nora Scott Kinzer, "Amnesia, Illegitimacy, and Braintransplants: Or the Sociology of the Soap Opera," unpublished paper, given at Third Annual Popular Culture Association meeting, April 13–15, 1973.

53. Astrachan, p. 62.

54. Kinzer, p. 2.

55. Anne Roiphe, "The Waltons," *The New York Times Magazine*, Nov. 18, 1973, p. 41.

56. *Ibid.,* p. 130.

57. *Ibid.,* p. 133.

58. Robert Warshow, "The Gangster as Tragic Hero," in *The Immediate Experience.* All quotations in this section are from this article.

59. Raymond Chandler, "The Simple Art of Murder," quoted in Paul Jensen, "The Writer: Raymond Chandler and the World You Live In," *Film Comment,* Vol. X, No. 6 (Nov.– Dec. 1974) p. 19.

60. *Ibid.,* p. 20.

61. All the following quotations in this chapter are from books in the Travis McGee Series by John D. MacDonald. All of these are Fawcett Gold Medal paperbacks. The ones quoted are listed below with dates and coded number to be used in the references below:

  1. *The Deep Blue Good-by* (1964)

  2. *Nightmare in Pink* (1964)

  3. *A Purple Place for Dying* (1964)

  4. *The Quick Red Fox* (1964)

  5. *A Deadly Shade of Gold* (1965)

  6. *Bright Orange for the Shroud* (1965)

  7. *One Fearful Yellow Eye* (1966)

  8. *Dress Her in Indigo* (1969)

  9. *The Long Lavender Look* (1970)

  10. *A Tan and Sandy Silence* (1971)

  11. *The Scarlet Ruse* (1973)

  12. *The Turquoise Lament* (1973)

The quote referred to here is from 4, p. 63.

62. 10, pp. 228–229.

63. 4, pp. 96–98; 3, pp. 39–40.

64. 4, p. 96.

65. 5, pp. 37–38.

66. 3, pp. 27, 29.

67. 7, p. 55.

68. 6, pp. 119–120.

69. 1, p. 112.

70. 9, p. 165.

71. 1, p. 47.

72. 5, pp. 46–47.

73. 9, p. 146.
74. 11, p. 246.
75. 5, p. 232.
76. 12, p. 87.
77. 8, pp. 252–253.
78. 2, pp. 28–29.

Bibliography

Books

Cawelti, John G. *The Six-Gun Mystique.* Bowling Green, Ohio: Bowling Green University Popular Press, 1970.

Fishwick, Marshall. *Parameters of Popular Culture.* Bowling Green University Popular Press, 1974.

Fishwick, Marshall, and Browne, Ray B., eds. *Icons of Popular Culture.* Bowling Green University Popular Press, 1970.

French, Philip. *Westerns: Aspects of a Movie Genre.* The Viking Press, Inc., 1973. 1974.

Hammel, William M., ed. *The Popular Arts in America: A Reader.* Harcourt Brace Jovanovich, Inc., 1972.

Huebel, Harry Russell, ed. *Things in the Driver's Seat: Readings in Popular Culture.* Rand McNally & Company, 1972.

Kitses, Jim. *Horizons West.* Indiana University Press, 1970.

Kuhns, William. *The Electronic Gospel: Religion and Media.* Herder & Herder, Inc., 1969.

Kuhns, William. *Environmental Man.* Harper & Row, Publishers, Inc., 1969.

MacDonald, John D. The Travis McGee Series, all published by Fawcett Publications, Inc. The titles and dates of original publication are: *The Deep Blue Good-by,* 1964; *Nightmare in Pink,* 1964; *A Purple Place for Dying,* 1964; *The Quick Red Fox,* 1964; *A Deadly Shade of Gold,* 1965; *Bright Orange for the Shroud,* 1965; *One Fearful Yellow Eye,* 1966; *Darker Than Amber,* 1966; *Pale Gray for Guilt,* 1968; *The Girl in the Plain Brown Wrapper,* 1968; *Dress Her in Indigo,* 1969; *The Long Lavender Look,* 1970; *A Tan and*

Sandy Silence, 1971; *The Scarlet Ruse,* 1973; *The Turquoise Lament,* 1973; *The Dreadful Lemon Sky,* 1974.

Nachbar, Jack, ed. *Focus on the Western.* Prentice-Hall, Inc., 1974.

Nevins, Francis M., Jr., ed. *The Mystery Writer's Art.* Bowling Green University Popular Press, 1971.

Nye, Russell B. *The Unembarrassed Muse: The Popular Arts in America.* The Dial Press, Inc., 1970.

Ricoeur, Paul. *The Symbolism of Evil.* Tr. by Emerson Buchanan. Harper & Row, Publishers, Inc., 1967.

Rosenberg, Bernard, and White, David M., eds. *Mass Culture Revisited.* Van Nostrand-Reinhold Company, 1971.

Warshow, Robert. *The Immediate Experience.* Doubleday & Co., Inc., 1962. Atheneum Publishers, 1974.

Articles and Papers

Baker, Charles. "The Theme of Structure in the Films of Robert Altman," *The Journal of Popular Film,* Vol. II, No. 3 (Summer 1973), pp. 243–261.

Brinley, Maryann. "Fathers and Daughters," *Ladies' Home Journal,* Nov. 1974, pp. 123–124.

Corman, Avery. "The Beginning of the End of Sex: The First Baby," *Cosmopolitan,* Oct. 1974, pp. 188–191, 219.

Engle, Gary. *"McCabe and Mrs. Miller:* Robert Altman's Anti-Western," *The Journal of Popular Culture,* Vol. I, No. 4 (Fall 1972), pp. 268–287.

Ezzell, Robert. *"Walking Tall:* Buford Pusser as American Messiah." Paper presented at the Fourth Annual Meeting of the Popular Culture Association, Milwaukee, Wisconsin, March 1974.

Gerson, W., and Lund, S. H. *"Playboy* Magazine: Sophisticated Smut or Social Revolution?" *The Journal of Popular Culture,* Vol. I, No. 3 (Winter 1967).

Jensen, Paul. "The Writer: Raymond Chandler and the World You Live In," *Film Comment,* Vol. X, No. 6 (Nov.–Dec. 1974), pp. 18–26.

Kinzer, Nora Scott. "Amnesia, Illegitimacy, and Braintransplants: Or the Sociology of the Soap Opera." Paper presented at the Third Annual Meeting of the Popular Culture Association, Indianapolis, Indiana, April 1973.

Lambert, Angela. "In Praise of Casanova," *Cosmopolitan*, Oct. 1974, p. 24.

The New York Times. Arts and Leisure Section, Feb. 24, 1974, March 30, 1975; *The New York Times Magazine*, Nov. 18, 1973, Aug. 11, 1974, March 23, 1975.

Sonerschein, David. "Love and Sex in the Romance Magazines," *The Journal of Popular Culture*, Vol. IV (Fall 1970).

Willis, Ellen. "To Be or Not to Be a Mother . . . ," *Ms.*, Oct. 1974, pp. 28–36.